THE
DATING MAZE

Brent D. Earles

BAKER BOOK HOUSE
Grand Rapids, Michigan 49506

To my parents-in-law,
Larry and Lillian Timmons,
for allowing me two marvelous
privileges—dating their
daughter, and marrying her

Contents

Introduction

Fear. Sweaty palms. A heart beating so fast and loudly that others surely must hear it. Saying dumb things at the wrong time. Wishing. Daydreaming. Trying very hard to be noticed. Disappointment. Fluttering feelings of love. These are a couple of handfuls of things young people experience and somehow endure during the days of dating.

At the mention of dating, ears quickly perk up. Especially those of teenagers and their parents. The questions and conflicts run in a never-ending stream. The puzzles and problems that arise can leave a family feeling as though they are stranded in a dark maze, with no help and no map.

I do not know whom the dating maze confuses more, the parents or the teenagers. Part of the confusion is due to the rapid changes in our society's moral values in the last decade or so. Traditional dating is drowning in a swelling tide of sexual freedom. Unfortunately, sex has begun to play a predominant role in today's dating lifestyles. Unfortunate, because there is so very much more to dating than physical attraction and "fooling around." More unfortunate, because sexual permissiveness has its price tag.

The price is high! In 1982 over 30,000 girls under age fifteen were pregnant. Today, nearly 30 percent of all abortions are performed on teenage girls. Since 1968, premarital pregnancies have more than doubled. Experts estimate that one out of every ten girls between the ages of fifteen and nineteen will become pregnant this year. The maze keeps getting darker and more bewildering.

A new venereal disease, herpes, threatens to infect our society to near-epidemic levels, unless we wise up to the built-in penalties of sexual promiscuity. Thousands of teenagers have already contracted this incurable disease.

Parents have got to rescue their teens from these danger traps that leave lifelong scars. Choosing to remain naive to a drug-infested world which has also gone crazy over sex is to doom the younger generation.

But parents need to help their teenagers in more facets of dating than just the sexual one—how to handle loneliness and not being asked out, how to start and hold conversations, finding things to do, how to deal with envy and jealousy and even popularity, how to cope with a broken heart.

Teenagers need to do a lot of learning, too! Understanding their parents is a good place to start. Not to mention: what curfews have to do with trust, what responsibilities car privileges involve, how to spend money on dates, and how to build friendships.

So, you see, dating is a maze with many turns and high complexity. But then again, it is a wonderful time of life, a great part of growing up. It offers chances for pure fun, laughter, and fond memories. It is where most of us find love and marriage. Maybe it is a simpler maze than we realize, if we know the right paths to follow.

1

Parents, Aargh!

Almost every adolescent vows, "When I become a parent, and my kids become teenagers, I'm gonna be more understanding. I won't forget what it was like to be this age!"

By age twenty-five, a great deal of maturing has usually taken place. Fifteen seems like so very long ago. The closest thing is tomorrow. And parents have finally gotten much wiser in the eyes of their offspring.

At age thirty, it is hard to imagine life any busier. The job is offering very rewarding benefits by now, in exchange, of course, for time. Time, "Oy-yi-yi," everybody wants time! And thirty-five makes thirty look slow.

Finally, the teenager has grown to full parenthood. Now, at age forty to forty-five, he has the chance to keep that vow. "But," he says, "things have changed so much since I was a teenager. Young people are so different today. We were never that way, were we?" A conflict rages on in his household. In the private quiet of his teenager's bedroom, a dusty old vow is being made: "When I become a parent. . . ."

You cannot imagine your parents making a vow like that, can you? They probably did; they just can't remember. What's funny is that when you get to be their age, you might not remember either.

Being a teenager can be traumatic at times. As one thirteen-year-old girl put it, "This is all a dirty trick. I can see it now; the day before I turn fourteen, the very day before, I'll die. I know I will. Because this age is a dirty trick."

Parents do not make things any easier sometimes. I used to think my parents lay awake at night, conspiring as to how they could mess up my plans, or embarrass me, or make my friends laugh at me.

They were always popping up with some ridiculous new rule that nobody else I knew had to abide by. If I came home a few minutes late, they would frequently go off like a smoke alarm looking for a fire. No two parents were finer detectives. My parents could not be fooled. Mom was constantly reminding me to put on clean underwear and comb my hair. Dad was a regular Sherlock Holmes. He would read the car odometer and figure up the mileage to and from the places I had said I was going. A one-mile difference could result in a living-room court session.

I felt like an excited dog on a short chain. The second I went running after some new fun, that ignorant leash would jerk my head half off. When this dog turned sixteen he decided to bite, but got quite a surprise when his parents bit back. This all made for some not-so-amusing growling matches.

What I failed to realize at the time was that my biting and barking were causing great pain. People who loved me dearly could not understand why their "little baby" had grown up to be so mean. I could not understand why *they* were not more understanding. On the other hand, I was not a bit interested in understanding them. Does any of this sound familiar?

I must have had a tremendous knack of making people nervous, because both of my folks said I was making a "nervous wreck" out of them. The only nervous wreck I can remember is the one I had when I ran a stop sign while throwing water balloons. Dad found no humor in it. And he helped me forget the funny parts at the time.

My mom seemed not to like any of the girls I liked, until after I stopped dating them. Then she would ask, "Why do you like this girl? She's not nearly as nice as the last girl you took out."

Then there was money. Dum . . da . . . dum-dum. Let it be said that I was very happy to get my first job. Then I could spend my money as I pleased. After all the necessary red tape, of course.

May I be serious for a moment? Sometimes I miss being young, at home with my parents. Sound silly? It's the truth. And why? I guess I realize now just how much my parents loved me, and how much they still do. That part of life was as new for them as it was for me. Maybe I feel like a cad for the unkind things I said and did. So I wish I could do it over, knowing what I know now. I'm sure I would change some things.

You are bright enough to read between the lines. There is no sense in saying and doing things you will regret later. Even if it is much later when you regret it. Besides, being the parent of a teenager is not all it's cracked up to be. So beware of dusty old vows.

An Inside Look: Honor your father and mother—which is the first commandment with a promise—that it may go well with you and that you may enjoy long life on the earth.   (Eph. 6:2–3)

Beatitude: *Happy are the teenagers who try to be understanding, for they shall be better understood.*

2

Curfews

Cinderella blew it. Her fairy godmother gave her a lenient curfew, and she got so absorbed with excitement that she forgot to watch the clock. When the chime rang twelve she beat it out of the palace so fast that she ran right out of one shoe. Too late! One fine carriage was no more than a plump pumpkin. The stately team of horses scurried off as the band of mice they once were. Cindy herself made a riches-to-rags change in moments.

Curfews. Now there's an unpopular subject. "Be home by eleven-thirty, and don't you be late! Or else, I'm going to ground you for four hundred and twenty-nine days." Ever hear that?

Did you ever notice that no matter how late the curfew is, when it comes time to go home, you still want to stay out later? Or that when you are having the most fun, it's almost time to go home?

Sometimes I think that's the devil's way of tempting and causing trouble. Too many people fall for it. Rules get broken. Parents get upset. Struggles for more independence are pushed unnecessarily far. And all over coming in too late. But new freedom is rarely won by irresponsibility. Think about it.

Your folks place a high premium on trust. Why not? Trust is one of the few things that keeps them going when they know you are "out there" with little or no adult supervision. They were young once, and they have not forgotten the pressures to experiment around with things. Frankly, it worries them. They've got to cling to a sense of trust.

Coming in late pecks away at that trust like a badgering woodpecker. It's not that they don't want to believe in you, but being disrespectful of their wishes for you to be in on time goes a long way toward shortening how far they can trust you.

That does not always mean you can buy a later curfew with extended good behavior. However, it might free things up a bit for extra-special occasions. Which leads to an important question: Do you ever think that a certain curfew is late enough? That after a certain time there really isn't much worthwhile happening? If so, what time is that and why? If no, then why is most of the normal world asleep at that time?

"*Unreliable*" is a terrible tag to acquire. People like this lose privileges others enjoy, because they do not show enough evidence of being able to handle more.

"But nobody's perfect," you say? You're right. I expect everyone is late sometime. That does not excuse the ones who always seem to be ten or fifteen minutes late. Nor does it excuse the one who could have called, but didn't. Called? Sure. Relieve the worries of those waiting at home. Calling takes only a second.

"*Don't.*" There's another unpopular word, but an important one. *Don't* make up lies to cover for being late. This is very stupid to do. Certain disaster follows when your folks find out the truth. Besides, God takes a dim view of lying. The common list of excuses is timeworn and weary:

"We ran out of gas on the way home."

"We had a flat tire just as we were heading back."

"My watch stopped and I didn't realize it was this late."

"We were hurrying so fast that the police stopped us."

"We were held captive in a UFO."

"We got lost."

"We had a hard time getting the car started."

"We accidentally locked the keys in the car."

Of course, one of these things really could happen. Whatever the case, if you're late, tell the truth. It's easier to live with and helps keep trust intact.

Back to our earlier question. What is a good curfew? Personally, for weekend nights I think eleven or eleven-thirty is fair for fifteen- and sixteen-year-olds. Twelve or twelve-thirty might be given to an older teenager who has proven an ability to handle the clock.

If you have a friend who can stay out later than you, ask your parents if he can come home with you when your curfew is up. That might be okay every once in a while. And it beats complaining about how "Elmer" can stay out later than you.

Learning to gauge the evening's fun against the clock is far from easy. In fact, it can be downright difficult. But it would be better than coming out to find your car turned into a pumpkin.

An Inside Look: There is a time for everything, and a season for every activity under heaven.   (Eccles. 3:1)

Beatitude: *Happy is the on-time teenager, for he/she shall be trusted.*

3

Cars

Sport cars are fantastic. I love them. A low sleek look, plush interior, a dashboard that says: "All systems go!" In fact, I just enjoy driving. It's exciting, and does provide a feeling of freedom—even power.

Don't misunderstand me. Cars fall way down on my list of life's necessities. Nor am I an advocate of wild, reckless driving. I am an even lesser fan of big shots who want to show off their masculinity with little car stunts. These things are not at all impressive.

Dating relies heavily on the automobile. Furthermore, parents rely on safe driving to return their cherished kids back to them in one living, breathing piece. Unfortunately, it doesn't always go that way. The compound temptations behind the wheel are unconquerable for some. The twistedness of their torn bodies leaves nothing but fragments of broken hearts.

The following clip was written by an anonymous teenager. It's a bit gory, but I think it makes a strong point. Please read it closely:

It takes seven-tenths of a second to kill a person in an automobile crash. Studies at Yale and Cornell universities provided a dramatic split-second chronology of what happens when a car rams into a tree at 55 mph.

At one-tenth of a second, front bumper and grillwork collapse.

At two-tenths of a second, the hood crumbles, rises and smashes into the windshield, while the grillwork virtually disintegrates.

At three-tenths of a second, the driver is sprung upright from his seat, his broken knees are pressed against the dashboard, and the steering wheel bends under his grip.

At four-tenths of a second, the driver's fear-frozen hands bend the steering column into an almost vertical position and he is impaled on the steering wheel shaft. Jagged steel punctures his lungs and arteries.

At six-tenths of a second, the impact rips the shoes off his feet. The chassis bends in the middle, the driver's head is slammed into the windshield. The car's rear begins its downward fall as its spinning wheels churn into the ground.

At seven-tenths of a second, the entire body of the car is twisted grotesquely out of shape. In one final agonizing convulsion, the front seat rams forward, pinning the driver against the steering shaft. Blood spurts from his mouth. Shock has frozen his heart.

He is now dead. Grisly to contemplate, and all so unnecessary. The difference between death and arriving at your destination safely is simply a matter of thinking about the consequences. Recklessness is foolish. Drive carefully and **live**.

That is not one bit fictional. I know, because I have seen the actual results firsthand—and they were even worse. One evening I stopped to help officers with a two-car head-on collision. It would have been enough to make a two-and-a-half-hour-long horror movie. Three girls in one car, one guy in the other. The guy was drunk. He sustained only a broken leg, thanks to his stupor and huge car.

The girls were not so lucky. The one in the back seat was paralyzed from the neck down.

The girl in the front seat on the passenger side was in a coma with severe head injuries. Her very long and beautiful blonde hair was matted with blood. But that hardly mattered, because paramedics shaved her head immediately, revealing a deep cranial wound. Emergency transfusions were begun on a stretcher beside the car. She went into cardiac arrest nearly every time they tried to move her. I will never forget the tinkling sound of blood and plasma bottles bumping against each other as doctors worked desperately to keep her alive. Finally, they got her to the ambulance, but she died moments after they closed the door.

It took twenty minutes to cut the metal away from the driver. She was already dead.

This wasn't written to gross you out, although I must admit it is shocking. Nor is it intended to make driving miserable for you. Driving can be and should be fun, but not reckless. So, the next time you start up, drive with care. It will make dating more enjoyable. Besides, heaven can wait.

An Inside Look: This is what the Lord Almighty says: "Give careful thought to your ways." (Hag. 1:5)

Beatitude: *Happy are the drivers who are careful, for they shall be "wreckless."*

4

Parked Cars

Cars can also be dangerous when they are *not* moving. When parked in a dark, secluded spot, cars can be risky business. Lives can be messed up in the back seat. No matter how romantic it might seem, parking spells trouble.

People rarely park in dark places to talk. If you want to gab, go to a Burger King and sit over in the corner away from everyone else. Better yet, go to either your house or your date's. Your parents will probably give you guarded privacy for getting to know each other.

Sounds dumb, huh? With today's backward morality, I am not surprised if you have been duped to think so. This I know—if you sit in a parked car to talk, it will be very hard to keep things from heating up. The atmosphere will be charged, almost magnetic. You are nearly certain to be drawn into the dread and tempting grasp of sexual impulse.

Parkers know this. Parkers-to-be are at least aware of it. So should you be. A special young lady I know is well aware of it, and she knows how to handle the problem. Once a fellow tried to take her parking. When the car pulled to rest in an out-of-the-way place she said, "If you're thinking about parking with me, forget it. I think you're a nice guy. Don't ruin it. I want to think both of us have more to offer than our bodies. Let's go somewhere and talk. I want to get to know you as a person."

A prude? No, cautious and mature. That might sound a bit tough to imitate, but it's worth the effort. By the way, this girl is respected by almost all her peers. She does not have a bad reputation, and she gets her share of dates. Someday, she'll make some lucky guy a wonderful wife. Keeping your head on frontwards is the whole key.

Come on. Admit it. In high school there are a lot of fly-by-night relationships. And that's not so terrible, is it? But do you know what's really bad? Young people who treat parking like a sport, because once the fly-by-night relationship ends they are soon out in the back seat with somebody else. Then, after another breakup, somebody else. And so on. Suddenly the picture has gotten ugly. Don't you agree?

Besides all this, do you know what parking really shows? People have something to hide. Parking won't work in broad daylight. Only at night. Parkers head for secluded nooks where the dark will hide them from everybody else. Is it for privacy, or to keep from being caught doing something they know is wrong? Maybe a little of both, but certainly not getting caught is uppermost in their thoughts.

Park is supposed to be a place where people feed pigeons, play on slides, and watch baseball games. Not what they do when they want to make out.

I know what you are thinking. *This guy is so corny and dumb, who cares about this stupid book anyway!* Right? Hey! I'm not trying to rain on your parade. Give me a break, and pay attention to what I'm saying. Really, I'm on your side.

On my side? Yes, I am. It would be too bad if you had to face some of the terrible consequences of careless, casual sex. Think about it for a while. Risky business may not be worth the risk.

An Inside Look: Do you not know that your body is a temple of the Holy Spirit, who is in you, whom you have received from God? You are not your own; you were bought at a price. Therefore honor God with your body. (1 Cor. 6:19–20)

Beatitude: *Happy are the people who become "no-parking zones," for they will never be used by others.*

5

Expectations

Twin fools. One expects everything to go perfectly, and the other expects everything to be lousy. Both kinds go on dates with an unrealistic attitude.

The first twin will be disappointed, because nothing is absolutely wonderful all the time. You'll hear the letdowns. They come in handfuls:

"That restaurant was nothing like what I'd hoped for; it was so ordinary."

"Yeah, he was real boring. I thought he'd be charming, but he couldn't even carry on a conversation."

"Her looks are deceiving. I envisioned a girl who would be great fun, but she wanted to talk only about herself."

"Some enchanting evening. Ha!"

"You can be sure of one thing, I'll never do that again."

Anytime you set expectations way too high, you are riding for a fall. Little things go wrong, and the evening rarely works out exactly as we had planned it in our dreams. Sometimes a whole night acts as if it's been cursed. Everything goes bonkers.

Now, some high anticipation is unavoidable. Especially on first dates. Or the first time out with that "special someone." Or on big occasions such as, say, the Sweetheart Banquet. But cooking everything up to be a starry, perfect night might leave you wishing upon a star that the night will hurry up and end.

Sure you are going to get excited. And look forward to it. You should. This is really a tremendous part of being a teenager. On the other hand, don't get so keyed up that a letdown will leave you hurt.

Oh, yes, and beware of twin number two. This twin cannot imagine anything coming out fun. What makes a person like this? Well, some of these types used to be ultra-optimists, but after getting burned several times they can see only gloom, despair, and agony. Others are just naturally negative in their outlook. Twin two's traits show, too, in his or her remarks:

"I would never go out with *that* person. How dull!" (*Go ahead and try, you old pessimist. You might get a pleasant surprise.*)

"Oh, who cares about that stupid banquet anyway?" (*What's the matter? Aren't you getting to go with the person you wanted to go with?*)

"I never have any fun." (*Did you ever think you get out of an evening what you put into it?*)

You see, this twin has built in what a psychologist would call a "defense mechanism." This hidden device—playing everything down—keeps that person from getting hurt. Unfortunately, it keeps that person from a lot of other things, too—such as trying new things, meeting different people, making deep friendships, and in general enjoying teenage life. Sort of a monster, isn't it? Maybe "defense mechanism" is an appropriate name for it.

So, what's the answer? If your hopes get too high, there is bound to be a pin stuck in your balloon. Then again, some people have no balloon at all. Take a balanced view. There's no sense in being one of the twin fools.

An Inside Look: Find rest, O my soul, in God alone; my hope comes from him: (Ps. 62:5)

Beatitude: *Happy are those who keep a balanced outlook, for they shall see more good times.*

6

Friendships

Why does everybody take dating so seriously? Well, almost everybody. I mean, a couple goes out on a date and the next day at school it's a "love affair." The importance of dating is highly inflated. And its purpose is greatly misunderstood.

Friendship ought to be the grounds for dating. Couples ought to go out because they are friends and like each other's company. It would sure beat this *Snow White-Prince Charming* escapade that so often develops.

Instead, girls may act as if every date is supposed to produce Mr. Right. Some guys act as if every girl they are after has got to be another Princess Di. What's the big deal? Whatever happened to dating just for the heck of it—for fun?

I remember this date I had when I was in high school. The girl's name was Amy. Good ol' Amy—she was one of the greatest fun dates I had. Now the word was out on Amy: she didn't "fool around," get serious, or date anyone steady. But she was one great person to be around. If memory serves me well, we saw *The Sting*, ate pizza, and laughed our heads off all night long. I think we went out one other time after that, but we were never anything more than friends.

Do you know why I think we had such a good time? No pressure. That's it. We could just be ourselves. We didn't have to put on some false front, or make a big impression. There was a friendly, laid-back, relaxed atmosphere. That climate makes for memorable times.

There is more to dating, though, than having fun. Dating helps you get to know a person better. After all, people are fascinating. That does not mean you should do an in-depth character analysis of your date. Just talk. Your conversation will reveal a bunch about you as a person, and vice versa. A new friendship is born. You will find out that behind the faces of some of your classmates are some pretty special people. They will find out you are one-of-a-kind yourself. This will broaden your understanding of people, and in general make your world better.

It's not as though you have to have a special boyfriend or girlfriend. Some people go all the way through high school without them and survive. And you can't do without friends.

Which reminds me of a question I am often asked—"Can guys and girls be friends, with no other strings attached?" My answer: in high school, absolutely! That's the problem. Dating is blown out of proportion. This is a time to find out about the opposite sex— not fall in love with it or with one person. There's plenty of time for that. As you get older, your "friendship" dates will grow fewer, and serious dates will increase. But then you will be more mature and more experienced with people. It won't be so traumatic that way.

I hope you get to go out with someone like Amy, at least once, or you're going to miss out on one of life's neatest experiences. That would be a shame.

An Inside Look: A friend loves at all times. . . . (Prov. 17:17)
Beatitude: *Happy are the "friendship daters," for they have found a secret treasure.*

7

Respect

Comedian Rodney Dangerfield is always asking in loud, exaggerated tones, "How about a little respect?" There are other words to describe "respect"—courteous, mannerly, attentive, civilized, cordial, and considerate. Does that help you get a handle on it? Good. Because respect starts at home. And I do not necessarily mean toward family members (though it seems crazy that we are often kinder to strangers than to our own kin). I mean a lot closer to home than that. With yourself. Yes—simple *self*-respect. Know what I mean?

You have probably seen examples of what it is not. Every school has a guy who slouches way down at his desk. Doesn't open his books. Won't pay attention. He tries to look as sloppy and unkempt as possible. If looks could kill, he'd have wiped out the whole school. Often he starts fights, bashes in lockers, knocks holes in bathroom walls, and gets kicked out of school. Many turn into drop-outs. And it isn't *always* a guy. You've seen girls like this, too.

What's the problem? No self-respect. Sure, on the outside

hangs a coat of steel—Mr. Tough Guy. On the inside lies a world of hurt.

The truth is that many teenagers battle with self-respect—only in other ways:

No self-confidence

Not really liking themselves

Embarrassed by their physical appearance

Afraid of what others think of them

Overly self-conscious

Ashamed of family status

Doubting self-value

The trouble is, it is easy to forget that we are God's creation—each of us. God majors in originality. So He makes individuals, and He wraps them in their own unique characteristics. In other words, when God made you, He broke the mold. In fact, He broke the mold with every person. We are all one-of-a-kind.

You need to see yourself as special. Unique. I did not say you were God's gift to humanity, so don't get the big head. However, everybody needs healthy self-respect.

What's this got to do with dating? Good question. Self-respect puts us on the track of respecting others. You see, when a person cannot get along with himself, it shows up in nervy disrespect of other people. If you don't care about yourself and what you think, why should you care what anybody else thinks. Get the message?

On dates, these kinds of people are animals. They want what they want. There are few mannerly gestures shown. Rude, blunt, and crude—that's all. They are takers. Too many times they can even take the other person's self-respect away.

Those who are interested in living up to the decency for which God created them avoid such dates and such attitudes in themselves. They dodge anything that could ruin their self-respect, or the self-respect of their date.

You know, there is no evidence that being ladylike or gentlemanly shrouds one with ugly labels such as: "Miss Prude."

27

"Goody-goody." "Better-than-everybody-else." "Holier-than-thou."
"Mr. God."

As a matter of fact, these people are usually the *respected* ones. Oh, I know, they may have snide remarks made about them. But, deep down, the slugs who say those things wish they were so well thought of by others.

By the way, courtesy even looks after people who dislike you. Remember, God says we should return good for evil. Such kindness softens hard hearts. Sometimes it helps other people make much needed changes.

What do you say? How about a little respect?

An Inside Look: ". . . Where is the respect due me?" says the LORD Almighty. (Mal. 1:6)

Beatitude: *Happy are those with self-respect, because they will be respected—and respectful.*

8

Popularity

Poor Charlie Brown. He wants so badly to be approved and well liked by his peers, but all he ever gets is humiliating rejection. Every time he gets close to becoming the hero, a last-minute blunder makes him the goat. And yet, ol' Charlie is pretty popular with us, because we know how he feels. Too often we have dreamed of being the superstar or reigning queen—only to sit alone, walk alone, locker alone, and go stag.

Unfortunately, there is only one homecoming queen. Only one star halfback. Only one class president. Sadder is the fact that these are the ones who get most of the attention. Many who are left out have their special qualities, too. While the few relish and bask in the bliss of "worship," the many look on in quiet desperation—"Why not me?"

Which leads us to a thought-provoking question. Is it a sin to want to be popular? Not unless it is wicked to want to be liked. Everybody wants to be liked by everybody. Nobody wants others to dislike him or her. That's mostly what popularity is—being liked by others.

However, there are some bad sides of popularity that can surface and lead to sin:

Pride. A person can get to acting high and mighty after being the main attraction for too long. Pride is a terrible infection for the spirit, and it produces some filthy characteristics: bragging, bossiness, snobbishness, arrogance, cockiness, egomania. The center of attention doesn't like anyone else to be on camera. So the swollen head mushrooms all the more as the camera stays on him (or *her* for the snotty, upstage girl). You have seen what I'm talking about.

Cliques. Leaving out others who threaten your "image" is cruel. Not everybody is pretty enough, or smart enough, or athletic enough, or best-dressed enough to make it to the big time. Right? Bunk. What's with this shutting others out of your group simply because they don't measure up to some empty standard? This is one of the dangers popularity brings that must be wiped out.

Power. Some people like the feelings of superiority that accompany favoritism. They enjoy being "over" others, and can become scheming manipulators. They want their way, and nobody else's. It's common to see these types entangled in a power struggle with their parents at home, too. They get used to being in charge.

"Yeah," you say, "but popular people get plenty of dates." Well, there's a bigger point than that to be made. Popularity can be a blight for dating. Cheerleaders and beauty queens can be awfully choosy about the guys who ask them out. After all, they wouldn't want to go out with some nobody. They have to be asked by some "hunk" or "stud." In turn, fellows try to use their popularity to score with a girl they figure wants a shot at recognition for dating the school jock. Sometimes they're right. There are girls who look at dating as a chance to zenith them to the top, if they can link up with a guy all the other girls are after.

Dating a particular person can produce sudden popularity. So some people play little games to bring them recognition from their peers. What they do not realize is that their reputation is at stake. Their unselective behavior is giving them a bad name.

Want a tip? Don't play the popularity charade. Just be yourself. Try not to worry so much about what everybody else thinks. Besides, they are worried about the same things. Nobody wants to be a Charlie Brown.

<dl>

An Inside Look: A good name is better than fine perfume. . . . (Eccles. 7:1)

Beatitude: *Happy are the openly friendly, for they shall be likable.*

</dl>

9

Age Differences

She's dating a guy who's twenty-two!"

"So?"

"Well, she just turned sixteen!"

Age difference is a common subject about dating. How many years should there be between a couple's ages? Should couples begin by dating people their own age? Is there ever a time when difference in age is unimportant? Is it ever important at all, for that matter?

These good questions are not restricted to teenagers. Who hasn't gasped at the fifty-four-year-old tycoon sporting a voluptuous twenty-three-year-old wife? A woman young enough to be his daughter? In turn, people are equally shocked when a forty-six-year-old woman mates with a twenty-four-year-old fellow. For the most part, May-December pairings remain rare in our society, because, I believe, age difference builds in some natural barriers to this kind of relationship. Most of these barriers involve maturity:

The Outlook Barrier. If you are a teenager, generally speaking, a person several years your senior tends to be interested in settling down. This very thing attracts young girls who are interested in feeling secure. Along comes this independent man, free and on his own, able to take care of himself. How alluring this can be to a naive schoolgirl so eager to be independent herself. (Of course, no one likes to admit being naive or immature.) An older fellow, say in his twenties, is starting to think about marriage and a lasting sexual relationship. He might be looking for a commitment. The younger teenage girl, seventeen or younger, is not really ready for any of this. Most will be frightened away from such relationships. The men, as well, seek someone with a similar outlook. However, since the danger exists for an innocent girl to be taken advantage of, watch out about age differences.

The Communication Barrier. An older person (by that I mean old enough to be considerably more mature) has experienced a good deal and usually has a broader understanding of life. While this suave sophisticate enchants a young person with flutters of romance, most teenagers are no conversational match for a grown man or woman of the world. Don't fall into false "love traps" over age's ability to charm. It is hard to have quality mutual talk in the dating relationship with someone much older than you.

The Interests Barrier. Some interests are age-proof, such as, do you think the Redskins will make it to the Super Bowl again? Or, who will be the next President? Or, what do you think of the space shuttle? But when it comes to specific interests, a person in the twenties is thinking about apartments, career, and life insurance—while teenagers should be thinking about English, winning the conference basketball championship, and if or where to go to college. Tossing aside the usual interests of young people often means tossing aside your youth. Later on you might wish you could retrieve the things you missed out on. By then, it will be too late. To be sure, age differences do make a difference.

"How old should the oldest guy be that I date?" is a normal question from girls. I say "from girls," because guys usually prefer not to date anyone much older than themselves, wanting to feel able to control the date and take unchallenged leadership. Back to the question. In my opinion, if opinions count for anything, high-school teenagers should date other high-schoolers. Perhaps a senior would be ready to date a person a couple of years older, depending on maturity.

After high school, however, the age-gap ideal becomes a little less important. Both parties are (or should be) more mature. After college, age differences become considerably less significant. Eight- or even ten-year differences are not uncommon. Nonetheless, I doubt we will ever stop disputing those twenty- and thirty-year spans.

Hang in there. You'll get older fast enough.

An Inside Look: It is not good to have zeal without knowledge, nor to be hasty and miss the way.   (Prov. 19:2)

Beatitude: *Happy are those who don't try to grow up too fast, for they will arrive at adulthood right on time.*

10

The Undate

Up until now I have not meddled much in your deepest personal affairs. In this chapter we are going to chat about a subject that confuses and upsets many teenagers. So, buckle your seat belt; we're in for a bumpy ride. I'm buckling mine, because I figure some of you will be mad at me before chapter ten hits the runway. Are you ready?

You know that 7-Up is the "uncola," right? It's the *un*cola because there's no cola in it. An undate is the date that has no date in it. What? The undate is the date you should never go on. It is not wise or good to date non-Christians.

As 2 Corinthians 6:14 says, "Do not be yoked together with unbelievers." Verse 15 asks, "What does a believer have in common with an unbeliever?" It would be terribly difficult to claim that such a blanket principle has nothing to do with dating. Believe me, the temporary pain this standard imposes is worth the major trauma it prevents.

Dating the unsaved casually in the early- and mid-teen years only serves to encourage it later when a relationship becomes more serious. It would be emotional misery to stand eventually at the brink of marriage with that unsaved person, very much in love, and have to decide: "Should I go ahead and get married, hoping he [she] will come to Christ afterwards—or painfully break off our relationship?"

I know you have what you consider to be very sound reasons for dating non-Christians, if the opportunity arises:

"It's just an innocent evening out, no big deal." Underlying that reasoning is a basic misconception about dating. Sure you're supposed to have fun. And there should be sensible liberty in choosing your own dates. But there is something else you need to understand. Dating provides a very important learning experience for you. Dating is where you find out what the opposite sex is all about. How does the opposite sex think, express emotions and ideas, act in different circumstances, and what does it want out of life? All the while you are having a great time, another person's way of thinking is being presented to you. Even the strong can have their faith undermined by the subtlest comments or the slightest temptation. There's no sense covering the possibility of a problem by using a sweet word like "innocent."

"But he [she] is a very nice person." No one said that just because some people are unsaved they become first-class candidates for prison. No one called them lunatics or immoral scoundrels. Many non-Christians are decent people. However, to the Christian, Jesus Christ is the focus of life and its pathways. A number of other factors influence the unsaved. Even in "niceness" an unsaved date could unintentionally influence your beliefs.

"Maybe if I date non-Christians, they will be saved." There are better ways of winning people to Christ than dating them. Now, if you are willing to limit your date *totally* to church services *only*, it would be a strong matter for consideration. I fear, though, that many use this excuse as an insincere proposition to have their way. If you are truly concerned about their salvation, witness to them. Don't date them, thereby signaling blind approval.

"What if I don't know if he's a Christian?" doesn't pose a big problem. Meet on safe territory. Tell your folks the situation and see if they will agree to letting him come over for a couple of hours. In casual conversation you can mention church and your interest in pleasing the Lord with your life. If he is a Christian, you will find out quickly enough. If he gets turned off, you will know he's not. It will give you an opportunity to share the gospel, ensuring that you get the best possible time out of your dating.

"What do I say when asked out by a non-Christian?" This is easier for guys, because they usually do the asking. Christian guys can just avoid asking non-Christian girls, or can initiate conversations to find out a girl's spiritual condition more easily. It may be unfair, but girls don't have this advantage. What should a girl say? You don't have to say something ignorant such as, "Absolutely not, you unsaved jerk!" or "No, my parents don't let me date non-Christians!"

Something like this might be more in order: "No, but thank you for asking. I'm flattered that you noticed me." He will be instantly clued in that something other than his quality as a person is causing the problem. If he is brave enough to ask what it is, you must be brave enough to tell him politely, "Well, I've decided to date people who feel as firmly about their faith in the Lord as I do. That doesn't mean we can't be friends." Then you've left the door open for witnessing. Sounds tough, and it is. You might miss out on a few dates, get some unwelcome nicknames, and shed a few tears, but you'll avoid agony later.

Let me conclude with this story: Recently a middle-aged man visited our church all alone. After the services I introduced myself to him and asked if he was married. He said that he was.

"Is you wife interested in spiritual matters?" I asked.

"Yes, she is attending a church of a different faith."

"Oh?" I asked. "Are you looking for a church?"

He chuckled. "No, we've been attending different churches since we were married over twenty years ago."

"I see," I said. "Do you mind if I ask a question?"

"No. Go right ahead."

"How old were you when you got married?" I asked.

He seemed puzzled by my question. "Well, I was nineteen, she was eighteen."

I nodded my head, thanked him for coming, and invited him to "please come back." I couldn't help but think that this couple never dreamed in their late teenage years that they would attend different churches for the next twenty years or so. Neither does a person imagine having a spouse that will not attend church at all.

But it happens all the time. Why? I think it begins way back there with dating guidelines. Something to think about, huh?

An Inside Look: So, if you think you are standing firm, be careful that you don't fall! (1 Cor. 10:12)

Beatitude: *Happy are the cautious, for they do not become casualties.*

11

"No"

What if you are asked out by a guy you are really not interested in? Does a girl have a right to say no? Should you go out only with people you are attracted to? If I say yes to the first question can I say no to the second? How can a girl say no without demolishing a guy's ego?

Tough questions. Assuming the guy is a Christian (don't forget the previous chapter), you have a couple of things to consider:

Friendship: Could it be a casual date with no strings attached? If it can be, then why not say yes this time. Get to know him. A date doesn't mean commitment.

Purpose: Why do you date? For fun? For love? For security? For escape? All of the above? Saying no simply because a guy is not Mr. Perfect misses the mark. Of course, I think you should have some freedom over whom you want to date. But if romance is your chief goal in dating, you may have a misconception about dating. Dating plugs you in to getting to know another person, as well as giving you some good times. People don't have to have a "relationship" to enjoy a date. A quick thoughtless "no" might rob you of meeting and knowing some special people.

Do you get what I'm trying to say? You don't have to go out with everybody who asks you. But you should have some reason for saying yes or no besides raw physical attraction or sex appeal. People are more than bodies and faces. So bear that in mind before deciding.

Now, about how to say no. There are several ways to do this. Some of them are kind, others of them downright rotten and cruel. Here are some ideas to help you form a style of your own (and a few "wrong ways to do it" are here to show you what *not* to do).

Thank you for asking, but we are celebrating my mom's birthday tonight. This is the "explanation no." Actually, it never says no outright and implies that under different conditions a "yes" might be the answer. This is not excuse making, mind you. If the answer is no and will most likely remain so, then don't feel that you have to justify it. An explanation invites another ask-out.

Thank you, but I have other plans. This is old reliable for most girls. In fact, some guys expect to hear it. If you really do have something else in mind for the evening, fine—even if it's a little something at home alone. But don't lie.

Ha! Ha! Ha! Ha! Are you serious? This is painful. Don't intentionally hurt a guy, especially one who is unsure of himself and vulnerable to insults.

It was nice of you to ask, but I think we should be careful with our friendship. This is for the guy who expects more of a relationship than you do. Perhaps you have already gone out on a casual date and he wants to get involved. This will slow him down.

I don't know; let me ask my parents. This can bail you out from a date you are unsure about, or from a guy you don't know at all. Ask him to call back the next evening; then tell your parents about your uncertainty. Ask Dad to say no for now. If the fellow is really interested, he'll try again. Should he be wrong for you, tell him no, "but thanks for the thought."

Every great once in a while there comes along a guy who can't take no for an answer. That is, you can't let him down easily. If he persists and pushes, and drives you nuts, then tell him no bluntly and ask him not to call again. This doesn't happen very often.

Keep a balance. Go out sometimes for fun and friendship. And sometimes because of attraction. But always plan to get to know your dating partner better on the date. Then you can decide if it should be repeated.

It isn't easy to say no considerately and comfortably but it beats feeling like a worm.

An **Inside Look**: . . .Let your "Yes" be yes, and your "No," no, or you will be condemned. (James 5:12).

Beatitude: *Happy are those who know how to say no, for they keep "no" from being a crushing blow.*

12

"Yes"

Sounds easy enough. Many girls are so anxious to be the center of somebody's attention that they wait with baited breath, ready to answer, "Yes!" So what's the catch? The old affirmative surely doesn't pose the problems that a negative answer does. Does it?

Not exactly. This part of the dating maze can be deceptive, because it appears to be so simple. Suddenly you have taken a wrong turn, entering the twilight zone. Follow these ideas and I think you'll miss the pitfalls:

Ask first. There is such a temptation to accept a date before touching down with Mom and Dad. Nothing can mess things up faster. Parents don't like to think they're being taken for granted. Saying yes and then getting Dad's approval won't work either. You need a green light from authority *before* going ahead. Failure to keep things on the up-and-up with your folks can bring sudden social disaster. I heard of one girl who accepted a date prematurely. To drive home their point, her parents refused to let her go. Embarrassing? You better believe it was. But first things first. That only makes sense.

Be sure. Don't blurt out a big fat "Yes!" that you will regret later. This happens to girls who haven't had a date for quite a while (maybe never). They're so excited they jump at any chance. Careful now. There is no need to compromise your standards. Trying to get out of a date you wish you had never gotten into can make life miserable. On the other hand, the prospects of a date your folks approve—and that honors God—can be thrilling to look forward to. So be sure.

Other plans? Oops! Don't tell me. You said yes and later remembered you had other plans that couldn't be changed. Breaking a date this way can be really ugly. The guy always wonders if he is getting the runaround. He may not come back for seconds, thinking you have drummed up an excuse to call off the date. This goof-up provides you with tense living. Avoid its happening by double-checking your calendar before saying yes.

Bearing these things in mind can bring you happier dating. And they won't be terribly easy to remember. You heard me right. When you least expect it, you are asked out. Wham! Your head is swimming, especially if he is Prince Charming. Calm down, or you are likely to answer too quickly.

One other thing I want to mention here. Voice language. What's that? Well, you've heard of body language—sending messages by body position. Voice language is sending messages by *how* we talk. Catch that? The tone of voice doesn't always match what we say. "Yes" is said different ways to mean different things. Guys are not goons. They pick up on this stuff real fast:

You want to go out with me? . . . Oh, yes! I'll go! The guy suddenly realizes he is soon to date a dipstick. Don't fall all over yourself saying yes. The guy might think you're brainless. Try this instead: "That sounds like a lot of fun!" or "Sure, I'll look forward to it." This sends a signal that you're glad to go, while the Mushy Marsha answer makes you sound hard up and overeager.

I don't have anything better to do. This is a horrible way to say yes. It sends out powerful radar waves. It says, "If anything better were available, I'd say no." Bad vibes. It leaves a guy hanging. He questions himself, "What's that mean? If something better comes along, will she cancel?" This date is already off on the wrong foot.

I guess so. What's this mean? Are you flipping a coin to make your decision? An answer like this can cause a guy to feel bad about himself. Let me tell you, his job is scary. Fear of rejection and all. An "I guess so," is not a smart way to answer.

By now you've figured out that chapters eleven and twelve go together. Sometimes you have to say no, so don't camouflage it with an "I guess so." At other times, thank God, the answer is yes. Just keep the process in order before accepting. Then clearly express your happiness at being asked. Then you can huddle with your girlfriends and act nuts.

An Inside Look: A word aptly spoken is like apples of gold in settings of silver. (Prov. 25:11)

Beatitude: *Happy are the ones who get to say "Yes!" and they should be considerate of others who rarely share that privilege.*

13

Personal Upkeep

The dad of a teenage boy expressed to me recently that his son was starting to show a big interest in the opposite sex. "How can you tell?" I asked. His answer was a funny one: "He combs his hair all of the time."

There is a lot of insight in what he said. When sexual awareness comes and interest in dating arrives, so does a wide-sweeping change in personal upkeep. Guys start tucking in their shirts, wearing cologne, and combing their hair. Girls smooth on the makeup and lipstick, worry about fashion, and try all sorts of hairstyles. Part of this involves maturing in self-awareness—becoming the unique you. The other part is plain appeal. We know that people look at the outside appearance. So, to get noticed, we try to look our best.

Is that wrong? Is it wrong for a guy to look and smell as good as he can? Is it wrong for a girl to fix up her face and try to show her physical assets in an attractive way?

Not at all. In fact, this is an important part of dating—and growing up, for that matter. Girls do not appreciate slobs. They are not usually attracted to some guy who could be the next hobo of the year. I don't think a sensible girl expects "best-dressed," but she is turned off by the crudeness of a smelly guy. She is smart enough to know that if you do not care enough to take care of yourself, you will probably not take very good care of her, either.

Guys are no different. They prefer their girls feminine-looking, sweet-smelling, and nicely styled. They don't really expect you to be the Perfect 10 (regardless of what the wicked morality of society says), but they won't chase the Total 0 either. A guy figures that if a girl doesn't care enough about herself to look her best, then why should he care about taking her out.

Now, there is a danger in putting an emphasis on the old bod, and forgetting inward beauty and radiance of spirit. For it is these that give outward attractiveness their life flow. The face fades when the heart is ugly. Nonetheless, I think it is good for us to get into the habit of taking proper care of our bodies. To try to look our best. Nothing says that bland is beautiful. Nothing says that sloppy is spiritual. So wise up and be neat.

I shouldn't have to ask these questions, but I will, because I know there are teenagers in every high school who need to hear them. Either their parents haven't taught them, or else they aren't listening. Here goes (save your laughing until I'm finished):

Do you take a bath every day?

Do you brush your teeth and use mouthwash twice daily?

Do you use deodorant?

Do you wash your hair regularly?

Do you change underwear daily?

Do you throw your clothes in the wash hamper when they get dirty?

Do you clean out your ears?

Do you clip or file your fingernails and toenails?

Do you shave (guys—faces; girls—legs and underarms)?

Do you wipe the sleep out of your eyes?

Do you try to prevent other possible body odors?

Neglecting these things can make you offensive to others. Put bluntly, you can really stink! If no one ever told you, allow me: when you approach young adulthood you begin to get adult odors. You have to do something about these critters or else you're going to smell like a garbage dump. Okay, I'm finished. You can laugh out loud now.

Here's the point. People with even an ounce of dignity take care of their total selves. Getting noticed is only a part of it, but one of the nice parts. There's a mirror in this tunnel of the dating maze. It invites you to check out your physical appearance. It then says, "Look deeper, at the real you." Well, how about it? Does the inside you need any cleaning up?

Good personal habits help the inside, too. Habits of prayer and Bible reading. Habits of church attendance and obedience. Then they shine through to make a better-looking outside you. Oh, no, not in sex appeal, but in genuine, lasting attractiveness.

Go ahead. Take a bath if you need one. Inside and out.

An Inside Look: The LORD does not look at the things man looks at. Man looks at the outward appearance, but the LORD looks at the heart. (1 Sam. 16:7).

Beatitude: *Happy are the radiant, for they shine inside out.*

14

Habits

It has been said that people could live twice as long if they didn't spend the first half of their lives acquiring habits that shorten the second half. Take notes, because this is the crucial time of life when many death-grip habits get you into a headlock.

How did this get into a dating book? Simple. Boyfriends often start their girlfriends on some powerfully habit-forming stuff, and vice versa. Please don't fold your arms and stare off into space. You have to be tough enough to listen to rough words if you are going to be mature. Hiding in a little shell serves only to isolate you from the cold, hard facts. Then again, some of you might be naive about these things. For your own sake, wake up.

Cigarettes are never glamorous. But look at the magazine and billboard advertising appeals. They make all the men look ruggedly handsome, every woman's dream. What's their gimmick? "Fellas, if you smoke, you too can be a *man*—the next Clint Eastwood." Other ads set a women in front of a you've-come-a-long-way-baby backdrop. She's a leggy, shapely model with every piece in the right place. Her message is: "If you want to experience the beautiful life as I do, light up some smokes."

To me this is serious business. Not just because of the obvious health factor, but also because I believe any time a teenager falls into the nicotine scene it's for attention—to feel important and to fit in. What a rotten reason to smoke. But, then, I doubt there are any good reasons.

That's only the tip of the iceberg, as the saying goes. Dates often turn each other on to pot and other drugs. Drinking falls into this "good time" category. Don't be fooled; these things *are* habit forming. Once a person gets used to them, it's a "drag" to do without them.

I don't have the space to share my life testimony (I'm sure you are glad to hear that), but before I gave my life to Christ I was into all that jazz. And I tried to get the girls I dated to try drugs or booze with me. Most of them did! I know for a fact that all of these external desensitizers are habit forming, regardless of what some so-called experts might say. If it isn't a physical addiction they produce, then it's an emotional and psychological one. In short, people who like to play with fire often get burned.

Most of the people who have gotten hooked admit that their habit began in their teen years. What was supposed to be fun became a ball and a chain—a master! By the way, I have heard the old standby, "I can quit whenever I want to." Trouble is that it is the *not wanting to* that shows just how much of a habit it is!

Let me close with a true story. One evening I was visiting in the home of a young couple in their middle twenties. The husband confessed that he was having a terrible time with pot. He was getting high three times a day—morning, noon (at work!), and night. His wife said she felt as though she should get high with him so they could "be together." I asked him if he would be willing to turn this sinful habit over to Christ.

His answer was sad. He said, "I don't know. I don't know if I really want to. Not that I like it. I don't. I hate it. Staying high is like a way of life for me. I can't imagine never being able to be high. I don't know if God can help me."

"When did you start?" I asked.

"I've been getting high every day since I was fourteen. Three times a day since I was sixteen."

He began as a teenager and still hasn't stopped today.

15

Time Tags

Don't jump the gun! Early in life we learn to cheat the calendar. Taking privileges and pleasures before it is your time to have them is a common error of our society. As a result we are a spoiled people, wanting what we want when we want it. Every generation grabs for things a bit sooner than did the last. The problem is, maturity has not yet been developed.

I am shocked to find so many sex-wise sixth-graders. By thirteen and fourteen, many of them are tuning in to dating and may have gone steady once or twice. This newfound attraction toward the opposite sex is okay, but I'm afraid too many parents let it get out of hand.

Beginning anything too soon leads to boredom. After a while, the next step in maturity seems necessary to bring back the fun-loving excitement. Pay attention now, because I'm not feeding you a sermon. This is the bottom line. Young people are experiencing more things at earlier ages. That's why we see thousands of teenage pregnancies every year. Thousands of teenage marriages. Thousands of teenagers dropping out of school to join the work force. Why? In a great percentage of the cases, the young people involved were spoiled by experiencing too much too fast. Result: it is taking more to satisfy them at earlier ages than ever before.

The question is whether you are really ready. Are you ready for dating? Are you ready for going steady? Are you ready for a job? Are you ready for bigger responsibilities? Are you ready for marriage? Be honest. This is no time for hasty childish answers.

I got a kick out of my four-year-old son yesterday. As I was mowing the grass, he came over and tried to tell me something. I turned off the mower.

Very confidently he said, "Daddy, I want to push the mower."

"All right," I said. "Go ahead."

He pushed with all his might. The mower didn't budge. "Well," his innocent blue eyes sparkled, "it isn't started. So it won't go. Start it!"

I started it and stood there to protect him. He pushed and pushed and pushed. He looked embarrassed and frustrated, so I put my hands over his and said, "Would you like me to help?" He nodded.

We cut out a couple paths of grass, and I could tell he was tiring. I shut off the mower and we sat down.

"Tired?" I asked.

"Yeah," he sighed, "it's too big for me."

I said, "You know what, Son?"

"What?"

"The day will come when you can mow the whole yard by yourself. Someday you might even mow other people's yards. Then after that you will have your very own mower to mow your very own yard. What do you think about that?"

"Well," he said, "first I have to get bigger."

That's what time tags are all about. Funny, isn't it? That a four-year-old can learn that in less than five minutes, but some people never learn. You'll never be sorry for waiting for teenage joys and adult privileges to come in God's prescribed way and time. So don't pull the trigger too soon or the recoil will give you quite a jolt. That's what is known as jumping the gun.

An Inside Look: My times are in your hands (Ps. 31:15).
Beatitude: *Happy are those who take life's steps one at a time, for they learn to walk more confidently into the future.*

16

Plans

Here's a "never." Never go on unplanned dates. I don't mean that every exact detail has to be planned—but stay away from "let's-just-go-somewhere" dates. You should know where you're going before you ever hang up the phone or say yes to a face-to-face invitation. Disorganization can lead to chaos, which can cause disaster. Couples can get trapped by sexual tension if there is no wholesome activity to fill their time together.

"Who should decide what we'll do?" is a familiar question. On first dates, the guy should usually know ahead of time what he is inviting the girl to do. When you call you should tell her the plans. For example, "How would you like to go out to eat Saturday?"

She answers, "Sure. Where?

You reply, "I thought Red Lobster would be good."

She responds favorably. Set a time. Tell her what you'll be wearing and where you want to go afterwards. Find out her curfew.

Another point in planning is to inform your parents. Tell them the basic details. There is no sense in having an "it's-none-of-your-business" attitude. Pleasantly sharing your plans for the night with them will put them at ease, and it will build a relationship of trust. But whatever you do, fulfill what you tell them. Lying about your plans to do something you think they will disapprove of is to invite God's paddle. Be sure, always be sure, that sin will be found out.

For second or third dates, I think it is appropriate for a guy to ask for the date, and then for the couple to plan the evening together. This is the joy of sharing and learning about each other's likes and dislikes. Go to different restaurants. See unusual sites. Seek variety.

Unplanned dating is most common with couples who date each other frequently. They get into ruts. After a while, it seems as though they've done everything that's okay to do. It gets harder to be creative. When this happens a big red danger signal ought to buzz off in your head: "Temptation is coming." Cool it for a while. Go out with others. But avoid the inevitable sin of a careless evening that has nothing else in it besides the prospect of groping in a secluded parking spot.

"How far ahead should we plan?" you might be wondering. For minor dates, a week or two in advance will probably be soon enough. For big shebangs, three or four weeks is best. If you ask too far in advance, you forget that things can change fast. By the time the date arrives, you may have changed your mind. An invitation on short notice is inconsiderate and will often be rejected because of previous plans.

Of course, things do not always go according to plans. The restaurant might be too crowded. The movie might be sold out. Something might make you late. So, have back-up plans. Then ring your folks and touch down. It takes off the pressure and makes for a much more comfortable evening.

Girls are sometimes bothered by guys with no plans. He calls and says, "What do you want to do Saturday?" Tell him you want to go to the fanciest place in town. If he says forget it, remind him that he asked. Don't settle for less until he comes up with some alternative plans.

In a nutshell, unplanned evenings out should never take place.

An Inside Look: May he give you the desire of your heart and make all your plans succeed.   (Ps. 20:4)

Beatitude: *Happy are those who plan their dates, for disaster cannot sneak up on them.*

17

Things to Do

I'm so bored. There's nothing to do. Even when I go out on dates, it seems bland. Everything just mashes together into one big boring routine." These were the words of a teenager. Ever feel that way? Have you ever been stumped about what to do on a date? Ever felt like the well of ideas ran dry?

What to do on a date depends on a lot of variables. Like:

What you enjoy

What your date enjoys

What is available

What your parents permit

How much money you can spend

How much time you have

What kind of date you want to have (a laugh-until-you-cry date, a romantic dinner by candlelight, a relaxing night out, a participation date, or a simple friendship encounter)

Whatever you choose to do should please the Lord. Since the Holy Spirit lives inside every Christian, we should be careful not to take Him places He would not want to go, nor do things He would not want to do.

God wants us to be happy. Do you believe that? He does. Some call God a killjoy because being a Christian forbids a person from really turning loose. There is nothing wrong with letting go to have a fun time, but a person who loves the Lord does not jeopardize righteousness for pleasure. And he does not feel deprived.

There is plenty to do on a date. None of these things has to be boring, if you are creative enough and excited enough to make it what you want it to be. You'll get about as much out of a date as you put into it.

Basically, there are two kinds of dates. There are entertainment dates, and there are participation dates. The entertainment date is a sit-back-and-relax date. There is not much chance to get to know a person on these dates. But they help break the ice for those who feel edgy about conversation. Sometimes they're great! A participation date is usually full of activity and offers a better opportunity for talk. Just be sure it involves the sort of thing both of you can enjoy. Here are some ideas for those whose well has run dry:

Entertainment Dates

A good movie (watch the ratings!)

Sporting events (high school, college or pro ball games)

A church service

Plays (school, professional, dinner playhouse)

Music concerts (school band, city orchestra, Christian, opera, ballet)

A rodeo or horse show

Special-events shows (Ice Capades, parades, and so on)

Participation Dates

Bowling

Horseback riding

Ice skating

Roller skating

Fishing

Miniature golfing

Going out to eat

Building something together

Washing a car together

Writing poetry together

Going on a picnic

Cooking your own dinner

Swimming

Skiing (water or snow)

Video games

Sledding

Boating

Motorcycling

Bicycling

Visiting a museum or art gallery

Hiking

Fair or carnival

Sightseeing

Window shopping

Tennis

Racketball

Ping-Pong

Youth-group activities

Working on a mutual hobby

School or church banquets

Visiting an airport (Watch planes and people. This can be really
funny. It takes a certain mood.)

Watching an old TV movie (if parents are around)

Playing a board game with another couple

Playing cards with another couple

Having a barbeque

Badminton

Volleyball

Painting together (especially fingerpaints)

Snapping photographs of nature and each other

Going to the circus

It would be easy to combine a few things into one date. For example, go out to eat and then go for a walk in a park. Some things are regional (ferry boat rides, trolley cars, sailboating, deep-sea fishing, mountain climbing, and going to the beach). There are tons more things to do, depending on your area and your imagination.

Climb aboard the "unbored" wagon. Let a team of wild horses drag out your inventiveness. Prove that variety is the spice of life! Go ahead. I dare you to try something new.

An Inside Look: And whatever you do, whether in word or deed, do it all in the name of the Lord Jesus, giving thanks to God the father through him. (Col. 3:17)

Beatitude: *Happy are the "unbored," for they have found that variety is the key that unlocks the door to good memories.*

18

Dollars and Sense

Money. That word is jam-packed with emotion—especially when it comes to dating. This part of the maze can be real disheartening. But it shouldn't be, because you don't have to spend a lot to have fun.

Extravagance might be impressive at first, but nothing can outdo the simplicity of sharing yourself. Your laughter and sense of humor, your tenderness and encouragement, your friendship and fellowship are all far heavier in value than painting the town *green*!

I remember calling a girl for a date when I was in school. At first we just talked while I worked up the courage to ask her. Somehow she got to talking about all the fancy, expensive places she liked to go. Then she started describing her elegant home and wardrobe. Suddenly I realized this girl was way out of my league. She placed a high premium on money to have fun. I did not. What's more, I could not! There was no money tree in my back yard.

Most guys don't have one either. So listen. Keep it simple. A date doesn't have to be an extravaganza. And if a girl is interested only in being "wined and dined," forget her. If a boy is trying to act like Mr. Money Bags all the time, ask to do something that doesn't require much money. He needs to learn to have sense about his dollars.

How much is a good amount to spend on a date? You will have to evaluate that carefully. How much can you honestly afford? Don't spend more than that. Even if you have the money, dates that don't cost much are often the most fun, because the financial pressure is off.

Occasionally, special big events come up. These dates can really cost, so you might have to save up. Renting a tux, flowers, and going out to eat can whop you hard. However, this is the exception to the norm. Usually, a simple dinner for two, gas money, and cash for whatever it is you will be doing is enough.

If you don't have any money, plan something that doesn't require any. Go back a chapter and look at the list. Invent something of your own. Take someone you can tell, "Hey, I don't have any money to spend, so let's do this. . . ." But be sure your date is the kind of person who knows you well enough not to think you're a cheapskate.

Can girls help with the cost? Sometimes. This has been such a touchy area, but I think it is changing. Guys usually like to do the paying. It's part of the macho image. So, it is probably not wise for a girl to say, "Let me help you pay for it."

What a girl can do is buy dessert. Or say, "Let me buy dinner this time, okay?" Or, "Since you're getting dinner, let me get the tickets to the ball game." If he says no, then he is tipping you off to let him handle it. Offer again later. If you sense that he doesn't like your suggestions, then let him pay. He may really prefer it that way.

On the other hand, a guy should not ask his date to share expenses. This is uncool. Asking a girl to pay her way qualifies for the stupid-of-the-year award. If the date wasn't her idea, why ask her to pay? If she offers, evaluate the situation before you say yes. Don't let her do all the paying. This is an important learning time for you both. Your money-managing foundation is being poured. Think about that for a while.

By the way, don't expect to get all of your dating money from your parents. Shoulder some of the responsibility. Earn a little here or there. Or use your own if you already have a job. Spending your own money encourages you to be more thrifty.

Overspending can bring regrets, but being a super tightwad can make you a nervous wreck. Relax. Spend what you can afford. Be a high roller on annual occasions (don't feel guilty if you can't). And don't let the old greenback dollar come between you and dating success.

Just have sense about your cents.

An Inside Look: For the love of money is a root of all kinds of evil. Some people, eager for money, have wandered from the faith and pierced themselves with many griefs. (1 Tim. 6:10)

Beatitude: *Happy are the "centsible," for every penny they spend is a worthwhile investment.*

19

Blind Dates

Have you ever heard of potluck dinners? Have you ever seen a grab bag? Have you ever played musical chairs? Well, they are about in the same category as blind dates.

A blind date is going out with someone you have never seen or met, through the arrangement of a friend. How good your friend is will probably determine what kind of date you are set up with. Many a dirty trick has been played with a blind date.

The question is, are they okay? Is it okay for a Christian to go on a blind date? That depends. Is the friend who is arranging it someone you can trust? Can you be assured that the date meets your standards? Will another couple be going along to make the atmosphere comfortable? Do your parents approve?

Provided these requirements can be met, and you don't mind taking the risk of "musical chairs" dating, then there is no reason why not. Just remember, you may feel like the person who couldn't find a chair before the evening ends. Blind dating usually has more letdowns than winners. Although sometimes they can be real fun.

I remember a blind date I had in college. My roommate was going home for the weekend and wanted me to come along. He was going to attend his high school's homecoming football game. But he already had a date, making me the third wheel. He wanted me to come home with him so badly that he had his girlfriend set me up with one of the hometown girls they both knew. Waiting for the evening to come was pure misery. I had absolutely no idea of what to expect—just the calm assurance of my sometimes ornery roommate. I told him at least ten times a day during the week before. "This hadn't better be a joke or I'm gonna break your neck." He would just laugh, causing me even more confusion. So I tried to get out of it, but he put the pressure on me. (This is all part of blind dating. The strain can be funny. It can also invite unnecessary problems that would never have come otherwise.)

The night we went to pick up our dates I was a nervous wreck. When the girls walked into the room I felt like covering my eyes and peeking through my fingers, then running if I didn't like what I saw. Suddenly, there they were. Both of them were nice-looking, but one was considerably prettier. I figured she was my roommate's girlfriend, so I cast my attention on the other girl. When I did she introduced me to her friend—my date! I was stunned! We all laughed. It turned out to be a fun night. My date was even prettier inside than on the outside. It was a casual evening. It never worked out for me to go home with my roommate again that year. I haven't seen the girl since.

Lesson: don't be expecting fantastic, romantic dreams to come true on blind dates. On any date, for that matter! Love, real love that is, must be cultivated over a period of time. Look out for love-at-first-sight expectations.

One other blind date I had bears mentioning here. A girl I was dating teasingly set me up with one of her friends. She went out that evening with another guy. Since we weren't serious about each other, it was no big deal. Her friend's name was Jane Timmons. I will never forget how taken I was with her from the beginning. As a matter of fact, after several years of "on-again, off-again" dating, I married her. Today we laugh about how we met. We tell each other it was "love." In reality we know that true love was a long time in developing. Now it gets stronger every day.

Why did I put this chapter in? Because one crooked path of the dating maze entices you to experience immediate love. It tells you that you must fall in love right now. It even says blind dates can be a fast ticket to romance. This chapter is here to say "Hogwash!"

Blind dates can be fun . . . sometimes! If all the specifications can be met. But you should not be writing the script of *Gone With the Wind* in your mind.

Remember, blind dating is a lot like musical chairs. You never know what's going to happen next.

An Inside Look: The god of this age has blinded the minds of unbelievers, so that they cannot see the light of the gospel of the glory of Christ, who is the image of God." (2 Cor. 4:4).

Beatitude: *Happy are those who are not always looking for love at first sight, for they will be able to see it when it finally arrives.*

20

Doubling

In tennis they call it mixed doubles.

Parents often start off their teenagers on dating with double-dates. Two couples together, that is. This is supposed to help protect against "ye old hanky panky." For sure, it does take off some of the pressure, but there is no guarantee better than a trustworthy young person.

Double-dating has its pros and cons that both parents and teenagers should be aware of. Which do you want first? How about the pros? I like to tell good news. Here goes:

Double-dates help conversation. Four people talking are bound to fill up more empty word space than two people talking. This can make things much easier for beginning daters. You have someone along of the same sex to talk to when you can't think of what to say to your date. You also get to know more people this way.

Some things are better with four. Activities like carnivals, bowling, minature golf, and swimming are usually a lot more fun in groups. There is just more excitement this way. More laughs, too, because there are two extra people who share in the goof-ups.

New friendships can be made. Meeting new people and getting to know them is dating's greatest gift. In this, double-dating can excel. But you have to be willing to open up and be friendly. This is no time to clam up and be shy. Nor is it a time to be huggy-faced with your date all night. Be ready for the new friendship opportunities that come. (PS. Later in life, after marriage, enjoying the fellowship of other couples will be a highlight. Double-dating will give you experience in building friendships with couples.)

Good enough. Makes it worth trying anyway. Now for the cons:

It has its pressures. Double-dates are probably a little more prone to wildness, at least in some ways. Like wild driving. A guy usually drives. Having another guy along might egg him on to drive faster, or do donuts, or make a risky pass. Junk pressures might be greater on double-dates—beer and pot. Not always, but sometimes. Curfews might also be harder to keep. Easy now, don't get wiped out by all this! Just be aware. Or beware! Whichever is more appropriate.

Couples can be mismatched. For instance, here's a couple who just met, doubling with a couple practically engaged. While these near-strangers are trying to get acquainted, the "lovebirds" are having a slobber session. This can be quite embarrassing.

All things considered, double-dating can offer some good experiences. Have fun with it. Make it the single most favorite double in the world.

An *Inside Look:*   A double-minded man, unstable in all he does. (James 1:8)

    Beatitude: *Happy are those who experience mixed doubles, for they have the chance for twice as much fun.*

21

Sadie Hawkins

Our school had a party once a year called "Sadie Hawkins Night." It was a chance for the girls to ask out the guys. What do you think about that? Is it okay for a girl to ask a guy for a date? Or is it wrong?

Don't go nuts on me now! Because in certain instances I think it would be acceptable for a girl to ask a guy. I am quite aware that this may send eyebrows raising here and there. I also realize this goes against the grain of traditional dating.

But why not? Maybe that is part of the reason why so many teenagers have sexual problems in dating. It is taken far too seriously! Rather than two young people getting together for friendship and "funship" sake, they are role playing. As a result the pressure is on for dating to be more than it should be.

Don't get me wrong. I'm not trying to create a dating revolution. There are those who feel that girls are forward enough as it is. What I'm talking about are special cases where a simple suggestion might be in order.

For instance, suppose we have two friends who know each other well. No big love affair or anything. Just friends. They are talking at school one day when he says, "Man, life is so dull. I haven't done anything the last three Friday nights in a row. And this Friday won't be any different. Guess I'll just sit home and watch TV."

She agrees, "No kidding. I haven't had a date in weeks."

"Me either."

What would be wrong with a simple suggestion by her in this case? Such as, "Why don't we go somewhere? Neither one of us is doing anything." I mean, what would that hurt? Nothing. And it would not be "wrong" either. Oh, it might take a little courage. But it would not be the end of the world.

Example number two. A big, once-a-year, senior event is coming up and two friends are without dates. He has not considered the possibility of taking "a friend." So why couldn't she ask him? Nothing brash. Just a simple, "Hey, you know what? We're both going to miss this. Neither of us has a date, so why don't we go together?"

You see, we have this rigid rule book for dating that says, "Guys ask girls. Girls have to sit back and wait." It must have something to do with the macho ego and the seen-but-not-heard female. But there's no biblical evidence to support it. I think fellows need to learn masculinity, and girls need to learn femininity. But a simple suggestion for a date has nothing to do with masculine or feminine. Unless! Unless it's a lovey-dovey date. You know, courtship and all. In these cases, perhaps it is best for the guy to make the effort.

However, this is the point. We are forcing romance by making it a "boy chases girl" or "girl chases boy" scene. There doesn't have to be a chase at all. Just a date. No love. No romance. No relationship. Only pure, wholesome fun.

If we could convince every teenager to go for this, hundreds would experience their very first date. As it is, they won't. Because there is this traditional voice that says, "Wrong! Bad! Don't do! Judgment will come!" It won't. If a couple went out on a perfectly nice date, and had some plain, old-fashioned teenage fun, would it really make that big a difference who suggested it? Of course not! Not unless somebody's making too serious ado about dating.

Most schools have a Sadie Hawkins event annually. At all the schools that I know of it is one of the most fun activities of the year.

Why? Because the girls finally get a chance to do something they have wanted to do for a long time without being made to feel ashamed about it. Once a year we say it is okay for a girl to ask out a guy. Silly, isn't it? All this rigamarole for a single date. It isn't a marriage proposal, you know.

Tell you what I'm going to do. I declare it Sadie Hawkins Year! Now anybody can ask anybody. See, you're still breathing. We won't all die. And guess what else? Men will still be men; women will still be women. You just wait and see.

Sadie would be proud.

An Inside Look: You do not have, because you do not ask God. When you ask, you do not receive, because you ask with wrong motives. (James 4:2–3)

Beatitude: *Happy are those who keep dating simple instead of serious, for they are free from the pressures of traditional matchmaking.*

22

Dancing

Fred Astaire used to dazzle people with his fancy footwork, flowing to the words, "The best things happen while you're dancing." I've got a feeling some teenagers are not going to like what I'm about to say. *The worst things can happen while you're dancing.*

Now for the big shocker. I'm not against dancing—between married people. If a husband and wife want to slow dance, or whatever, in the privacy of their home, that's fine. Some of the old-time ballroom dancing presents a certain romanticism. But we both know that the dancing of today is far from any of this.

Tell you what. I will give you a few reasons why I believe dancing is a poor activity to get involved in, and when I'm finished you can jot down on a separate piece of paper everything that is *good* about it. Catch that? I did not say to list what you *like* about it, but what's *good* about it.

Here are my gripes against dancing:

The music. Almost all dancing by young people is done to rock music. There is nothing worthwhile about hard rock music. Scores of the musicians are into drugs. They sing about such things as immoral sex, satanism, murder, hate, drugs, rebellion, and death. Many groups are using back-masking, a lower-level recording played beneath the actual rock song. The listener's subconscious can pick up these often blasphemous messages. Some groups admit this openly and even go so far as to state it on their album covers. At rock concerts every kind of wickedness takes place. I know, because I attended them before turning my life over to Christ. I saw people higher than kites, out of their heads, unable to walk or talk. I saw people having sex in plain view of others. I saw people taking their clothes off and throwing them into the air. This might seem funny, but it isn't. It's very sad. So the music alone is enough to grind today's dancing to a halt.

It is sexual. Some of the most lewd actions occur on America's dance floors. This is so obvious that I wouldn't be able to believe it if somebody disagreed with me. Guys glue their eyes to the gyrating hips of every female dancer that catches their attention. Even in innocence, girls are observed like performers a burlesque stage show. In our day of sexual wildness, the girls watch a guy's torso just as closely. It all promotes a sexual tension that is bound sooner or later to seek a release. Couple that with the music which encourages immorality and you have a disaster looking for a place to happen! Listen to me. It is stupid to think that two healthy, curious people can rub against each other all night without getting excited. Not to mention the raging conflict set off in their thoughts. Dancing breaks down the defenses. Anybody who does not expect the often-impure result is blind.

It does not glorify God. You know, even the silliest activities can have some merit. Spiritual lessons can be learned from wholesome dates. Not from dancing. Not as it is today. It is not *clean* fun. It is unspiritual and ungodly. There is nothing in hard rock music or sexual slithering that can help you as a Christian. Nothing about it makes you a better person. Nothing about it helps you get to know other people better.

You might think this is just my opinion, but I could easily back up these beliefs with God's Word. I think we can safely say that if Jesus were here today, He would not participate in today's dancing or condone it as a dating activity. If you saw your pastor dancing a hot little number with a young girl dressed in tight silver satin pants, you would be ashamed of him. You see, it just isn't the kind of thing to do, for people who love the Lord.

I hope we are still friends, because I was not trying to make you mad. I was just sharing the raw facts. I hope you were able to take it.

Now, go ahead and make your list of the worthwhile things about dancing as a dating activity. If you can think of one honest-to-goodness redeeming quality about dancing to hard rock music, you will have done better than I could.

An Inside Look: Do not give the devil a foothold.   (Ephesians 4:27)

Beatitude: *Happy are those who dance to the sound of a different drummer, for they avoid happiness-threatening danger.*

23

Partying

A few years ago, a popular heavy metal rock band screamed out these words in "nightmarish" repetition: "I want to rock-and-roll all night and party every day." No, this is not another chapter against the evils of rock music. It is about another growing problem among young people.

It is estimated by experts that well over 90 percent of all teenagers will experiment with alcohol. In excess of 80 percent will get drunk at least once, and over 50 percent will drink regularly. As many as 10 percent might develop a drinking problem! Can this be?

Partying seems so natural. It is sweeping across our country with a frightening popularity. So many teenagers cannot wait from one weekend to the next to have a "party." By this term, they mean a gathering where alcohol is consumed. Usually beer. Other partying occurs by teenagers in bars and nightclubs designed especially for them. This is the extent of dating life for crowds of young people. A drunken bash!

This is a real problem. Why? Because almost every teenager I have talked to about drinking says something like this, "Hey, I only do it for fun. Everybody does it." There is more to it than that. Anytime people start dragging in outside stimulants (alcohol is actually a depressant in large quantities) to have fun, something is wrong. I know there is something wrong when I hear the moans and groans of teenagers upset at the prospect of not being able to "party" all-out. What is it that's wrong? Why do teenagers party? What are the real reasons beneath their desire to drink?

Tension at home. Quite often, young people caught up in the party cycle are unhappy at home. Alas! The great escape! Sure, it happens all the time. Hostility comes at home, maybe a big blowout. Result: teenager tries partying to get over the blues. This is a poor way out. It teaches you to run away from trouble instead of facing it head on. If you have problems, a big party might help you forget for a while, but it will not make them go away, and it cannot teach you how to handle them in a constructive way.

Thrill seeking. This might be the biggest lure of drinking today. It seems exciting! One of the common complaints of Party Hardy's is: "Life is so dull and uninteresting." Many teenagers drink for the thrill of it. They are bored and dissatisfied with life in the real, everyday world, so they turn to an escape. Hoisting beers.

Group pressure. "Everybody else is doing it." Right? Just to fit in, some teenagers will gulp down beer, in spite of the fact they dislike the taste and certainly don't want to get drunk. They feel drinking is worth it to avoid the uneasiness and embarrassment of saying, "No, thanks."

Unspiritual attitude. The teenager who wants God's will in his or her life knows that partying is far from helpful. They see it as the degrading activity that it is. The person, though, who could care less about what God thinks chases the thrill of the moment. He gives no thought to the future, only to the party itself.

These are the real reasons teenagers drink. Are you caught in this trap? Is partying a big part of your dating life? Hard to believe, isn't it? That people can get so easily wrapped up in the week-to-week rush of another party.

Get this, too. All sorts of problems make themselves bed-fellows with drinking. Fast on the heels of drinking is wild abandon, immoral sex, further problems at home, and car accidents. Does that sound like the way to enjoy life?

Don't let this be a part of your dating life. God wants true satisfaction for you. He wants your dating years to hold some happy memories. Rock-and-rolling all night and partying every day cannot be the answer.

An Inside Look: Wine is a mocker and beer a brawler; whoever is led astray by them is not wise. (Prov. 20:1).

Beatitude: *Happy are those who don't find their excitement in the bottom of a bottle or can, for their thrills don't make them wake up feeling like a loser the next morning.*

24

Sexiness

How should a girl go about getting a guy's attention? The world says, "Sex appeal!" There is a barrage of products and clothing on the market to draw out the sexiest you. One commercial seductively teaches, "Part of the art of being a woman is knowing when not to be too much of a lady." What do you think about sexiness? Is it okay for girls to dress up in the sexiest fashions?

Here is what a teenage guy asked me a few weeks ago, "What are girls thinking about? They wear their jeans so tight that nothing is left to the imagination. A lot of girls don't wear a bra. They wear their sweaters a size too small. Some of the swimsuits look like sexy nightwear. Now you tell me how I'm supposed to keep from looking!" I couldn't answer him.

How about it, girls? Do you think the push of the fashion industry is to make you sultry and irresistible? Do you think that people who make clothes are telling you to look sexy if you want to be seen and admired?

Let's face it. Our society has its eyes bugged out over beautiful women. TV and movie stars who flaunt their figures in the scantiest outfits get the most attention. Sex symbols get ratings, sell tickets and lurid posters. They make the covers of women's magazines and are idolized by teenage girls. No wonder sexiness sells. It's what we emphasize in the media.

But listen. A girl should not have to dress sexily to get attention. The natural beauty of youth and the vibrancy of a peppy personality are far greater assets. Don't feel as if you must cram yourself into a pair of tight jeans to get noticed.

Whenever girls use sex appeal as a means of getting dates, they need to realize that their date will be looking for sex. After all, it was the body that got him to look. What do you prefer to emphasize? Which is the real you? Is it your body or your personality?

Am I saying that you shouldn't look good? No, not at all. Look your best. Curl your hair into a nice, flattering style. Use makeup and lipstick if it will help. Select dresses, skirts, or pants that are attractive. But don't hang yourself out like a piece of meat. Don't be cheap-looking.

There are a few girls (I say "a few" because most girls are not like this) who become labeled "tease." A girl gets that label because of the way she dresses and acts toward the opposite sex—trying to excite them and get them to look her over. This is a horrible reputation to have.

What kind of clothing causes this problem? I mean, how can you avoid looking immodest? Maybe this will help:

Reject pants that fit very tight.

Beware of dresses that have long slits up the leg, or cling excessively to the body.

Watch out for thin fabric with a see-through look.

Avoid plunging necklines.

Don't choose items made obviously and strictly to show off the alluring lines of your figure.

Believe it or not, that still leaves a lot of clothing to choose from. There are great-looking clothes that don't sell your body or sexualize you. Part of the art of being a young woman is knowing how to dress like a lady.

An Inside Look: Your beauty should not come from outward adornment. . . . Instead, it should be that of your inner self. (1 Peter 3:3–4).

Beatitude: *Happy are the modest, for the value of their virtue cannot be bought by sex-ridden fashions.*

25

Good Looks

In 1975 Janis Ian sang a haunting song that got across a message of sad reality. Some of the lyrics went like this: "I learned the truth at seventeen that love was meant for beauty queens. . . . Those of us with ravaged faces, lacking in the social graces, desperately remained at home, inventing lovers on the phone who would call and say come dance with me. . . ."

Our society teaches children early that good looks are more preferable than plainness or ugliness. This is even pointed out in childhood stories. Take Snow White. We are constantly confronted by the question of the wicked queen: "Mirror, mirror on the wall, who's the fairest of them all?" Then there's Sleeping Ugly. Oops! I mean Sleeping Beauty. Don't forget Cinderella, the drab, cinder girl who made the greatest rags-to-riches headlines of all time!

Even the animals get drawn into this fiasco. How about poor Dumbo the Elephant. You know, the one with the floppy ears. Then, of course, there's Rudolph the Red-Nosed Reindeer, whose strange beak made him a freak. The topper is the Ugly Duckling. Ever wonder why the story could not have been about a cute duck instead?

By age twelve most people are able to assess the worth of their physical attraction. Those who lack handsomeness or fail to "blossom" are often heartbroken over their rejection. Don't think the physically imperfect have not heard about their flaws. Cruel people are quick to intimidate those who are too short or too tall, too fat or too thin, or sway-backed or big-nosed or big-eared or freckled, or whose hair is too curly, too straight, too thin, or red.

Maybe you have experienced your fair share of ridicule and vicious verbal torture. It hurts, doesn't it? Like poison, the terrible words of teasing can bring tears of embarrassment to an already shattered ego. It leads many girls to question, "God, why couldn't You have made me prettier?" Believe it or not, guys can also be trapped in this confusing maze of self-doubt and battle disappointment over their looks. We care what others see when they look at us. We want to be approved. When we are not because of how we look, it can be devastating.

In his book, *Hide or Seek*, Dr. James Dobson discusses the beauty-cult mentality of America. He shares the unforgettable memories of some people who experienced feelings of being an outcast. He also reproduces this letter from a fourth-grade girl. It reads:

Awful Janet
Your the stinkest girl in this world. I hope you die but of course I suppose that's impossible. I've got some ideals.
1. Play in the road.
2. Cut your throad.
3. Drink poison.
4. get drunk.
5. knife yourself.
Please do some of this *you big fat girl* [ital. mine] we all hate you. I'm praying Oh please lord let Janet die. Were in need of fresh air. Did you hear lord cause if you didn't well all die with her here. See Janet *we're not all bad.*

From Wanda

There's nothing funny about that. Imagine being ten years old and finding this note on your desk. As you read it, the whole class laughs at you and runs out to recess—leaving you there all alone. Pure agony.

Here's what I know. I know some of you are going through a private hell of your own right now. You are down on yourself because you are not a "beauty queen" or a Handsome Harry. Some physical flaw or facial acne or weight problem or something else has forced you into the shadows, away from your classmates. You are wishing that high school would hurry and be over. Week follows week and still no date.

May I share a dear truth with you? Please don't shrug it off. You are very precious to God. He made you for Himself and His glory. He is aware of cruelty in the world of glamour. He knows your pain. Would you do this? Tell God how you feel. Ask Him to take control of your burden. Ask Him to lead in your dating life as He sees fit. Draw from His strength. Most of all, realize that you are extremely valuable, because you are His special creation.

For those who may be fond of their looks, here are five words of truth: beauty is only skin deep. There is much more to personhood than the skin you see in the mirror. Pride over good looks is dumb, because your basic makeup was not created by you. It was done by God in His works with genetic codes and in His wisdom. Develop the real you before the world convinces you that being one of the beautiful people makes you better than others. People who think like that are the true ugly ducklings.

An Inside Look: Charm is deceptive, and beauty is fleeting; but [one] who fears the LORD is to be praised. (Prov. 31:30).

Beatitude: *Happy are those who accept themselves and others as they are, for they are ready to work on self-improvement with hope.*

26

Loneliness

In 1942 a country-western singer made famous a sore-at-heart ballad. His name? Hank Williams. His own life full of unhappiness, Hank Williams sang these words from the personal distress he faced:

> Hear that lonesome whippoorwill?
> He sounds too blue to fly
> The midnight train is whining low,
> I'm so lonesome, I could cry.

Everybody has felt the sting of loneliness. None so much as the teenager going long without dates, or having difficulty building good friendships. Chances are, you have felt lonely once or twice.

I read that there was an ad placed in a Kansas newspaper recently. The ad said: "*I will listen to you talk for 30 minutes without a comment for $5.00.*"

Sounds crazy, I know. But would you believe that the person who placed the ad was soon receiving ten to twenty calls per day?

That just goes to show how many lonely people there are out there.

Going out at this age is very important to you. Staying home all the time can be disheartening and depressing. It makes a person wonder, "What in the world is wrong with me that I can't get a date?" The pressure this creates can drive a person to make friends with the wrong kind of groups. Anything for acceptance. Look out for this. There is no lonelier road than the one a prodigal walks on.

Loneliness is no respecter of persons. It strikes at will. Even "beautiful people" feel its pangs. I know of a few girls so pretty and so smart that guys feel intimidated by them. In fact, they are wonderful girls, but cannot get dates because their beauty works against them. Talk about feeling lonely!

I know a very handsome guy, six foot-four, and in tiptop shape. A star basketball player, he battles with loneliness because he is too shy to ask a girl for a date. All the love-stricken girls would jump at the chance to cure his case of the blues. But he is the prisoner of his own loneliness.

There is the young person who just moved to a new area. Adjusting has been difficult, the loneliness unbearable. There is the couple who broke up about a week or two ago. Both are forlorn in getting over it. Or there is the girl who did not get asked to the Homecoming Banquet, or the guy who just got turned down after mustering up enough confidence to ask. When you least expect it, loneliness strikes. Uninvited, it can be hard to chase away.

It would be dumb for me to say, "Aw, cheer up! Tomorrow's another day. Things will get better." Some of that is true, but it is no help right now. If I could find a cure for loneliness, I would bottle and sell it. It would put me on Easy Street for the rest of my life. I don't have a cure, but I have an ointment. What?

Jesus. That's right. He knows exactly how you feel. When He was being carried away to lonely Golgotha, every one of His friends and disciples fled. He was all alone. As He died for our sins, so that we could be forgiven and have salvation, even the Heavenly Father turned from Him. Jesus understands how you feel. He sympathizes and He cares. He wants to heal your hurt. He is called the Balm of Gilead, because He soothes our wounds. Lift your eyes up—off yourself—and look to Jesus. Ask Him to give you strength and new hope. Don't wallow in self-pity.

Even the lonesome whippoorwill sings a touching melody.

An Inside Look: There is a friend who sticks closer than a brother. (Prov. 18:24)

Beatitude: *Happy are those who enter into loneliness at least once, for they have the privilege of knowing a small part of the suffering our Lord experienced.*

27

Envy

Have you ever looked at the benefits another person is enjoying and wished that you could enjoy those things too? Have you ever thought that things went smoothly for other people your age and wondered why they did not go nearly so well for you? Have you ever tried to emulate someone, perhaps one of your classmates, in hopes that some of his or her success would come your way? Have you ever wished that you could be someone else?

If the answer is yes to any of these questions, then you have already met one of life's continual temptations. Just in case, let me introduce you. Meet Mr. Envy, Father of Covetousness. Envy begins with empty hands and concentrating on what appears to be the full hands of others. Envy asks, "Why not me?"

It has been said that when you feel yourself turning green with envy, you are ripe for trouble. It is sort of like the woman who says she is allergic to furs. Every time she sees a friend wearing a new mink coat she gets sick.

Envying people for who they are or what they have is silly. Every person has something no other person has. It would be far better to spend your energy developing the qualities *you* have, so that they can become outstanding, than to waste yourself in envy.

Recently, a teenage girl was ripping into one of her peers. Her venom flowed from envy, and I told her so. She said, "Her? She changes boyfriends so often none of them gets a chance to like her. I guess she thinks she's something because so many of the boys chase her. I'll tell you one thing, if I had a boyfriend, I wouldn't treat him like that."

Did you catch the key phrase that tipped off her enviousness? *If I had a boyfriend. . . .* She saw her empty hands and the other girl's full hands. Deep down she was thinking, "That girl has so many boyfriends and so many dates, why can't I have just one?" Mark it down, a person usually criticizes the individual whom he inwardly envies.

Let's admit it, though. At times we have all secretly felt just like this girl. Sometimes not secretly. We have grumbled about our misfortunes before and found the success of others hard to swallow. We have been impatient with God and tried to place blame somewhere. Haven't we?

Watching others can be dangerous business. It leads to comparisons. Comparisons are a bummer! They either tell you that you're a bit better off than someone else, or that someone else is better off than you. The Christian is constantly reminded in the Bible to keep his eyes on Christ. Jesus alone is our example, the One we should seek to imitate.

Does envy have a stranglehold on you? If so, confess it to the Lord. Get the heavy load off your heart. Ask Him to remove this cold creature from your thoughts. Ask Him to replace envy with gratitude for your blessings. How transforming—like a breath of fresh air! Take a whiff. A deep one.

An Inside Look: A heart at peace gives life to the body, but envy rots the bones. (Prov. 14:30)

Beatitude: *Happy are those who don't envy others, for they are the only ones worth envying.*

28

Jealousy

An ancient proverb has it: "Jealousy is the injured lover's hell." Or as Alfred, Lord Tennyson wrote: "Jealousy in love, that is love's curse."

Jealousy is sister to envy. Envy mourns its empty hands in light of other's full hands. Jealousy fears losing what it already has. In fact, it grows into possessiveness. It seeks to control people like objects. Anytime a rivalry crops up over a position or possession or person who falls under your "jurisdiction," jealousy is rearing its ugly head.

Most jealousy over people is way out of line. I have watched guys go nearly berserk whenever another guy so much as said Hi! to their girlfriends. I have seen girls give vicious iceberg stares at other girls who even smiled at their boyfriends.

What is really at the heart of jealousy? Where does it come from? Why would we treat any person like a toy we don't want the other children to play with? Here are three big reasons. Check them out. See if they fit your situation.

Insecurity. This is the main culprit. A person you can count on away from home provides security. A boyfriend/girlfriend meets that need. Jealousy keeps sending warning signals in your mind: "Protect him or you'll lose him; then you won't have anyone. You'll be all alone." Beneath that insecurity is fear. Fear of having no one. Fear of losing someone you care about. Fear of what others will think if your "love" is stolen. It is common for people to have this kind of jealousy over regular friends. As a girl told me yesterday, "I'm a one-friend-at-a-time person. And I don't like anybody else horning in on my friends. It makes me mad [jealous] to see my friends talking to other people when I'm not included." That is insecurity! Linus, the *Peanuts* character, carries a blanket to solve his insecurity. Some of us carry people.

Selfishness. Within the heart of jealousy is a voice whispering, "Don't risk being hurt, no matter what!" Jealousy cares about one person only—self. It doesn't care if your girlfriend was just being nice to another guy. It doesn't want your boyfriend to meet other girls, because they might take him away from you. It doesn't want your friends to widen their circle of friendship, because you might not get as much attention. Jealousy is plain old selfish!

Distrust. Jealousy believes people will turn on you. When it gets out of hand, jealousy is almost paranoid. It yearns to make you think the worst about people you care for. It conjures up all sorts of lies to question your closest friends about. It tries to box people into your little world, because jealousy fears that if they are let free, they might drop you. Jealousy basically says, "Trust no one but yourself."

What a cruel word is jealousy! What a terrible trait to have! Saddest part is that jealousy gone wild drives people away. Nobody likes being held in the panicked, fierce grip of another, no matter how close the relationship.

It's time Linus gave up his security blanket.

An Inside Look: God has said, "Never will I leave you; never will I forsake you." So we say with confidence. "The Lord is my helper; I will not be afraid. What can man do to me?" (Heb. 13:5–6)

Beatitude: *Happy are the trusting ones, for their security is in the One who never leaves us.*

29

The Phone

Howard Cunningham, father of Richie and Joanie on the famous TV comedy "Happy Days," once commented to The Fonz about Richie's constant use of the telephone, "Alexander Graham Bell gave us the telephone, but teenagers took us one step further—they gave us the busy signal."

The phone is a convenient little gadget. Especially for teenagers, because they can have conversations without actually facing the person. It is a lot easier to talk on the phone, more relaxed. Don't you think? It is definitely easier for a guy to ask a girl for a date over the phone than in person. Rejection is not as hard to take. Fear can be covered. The phone also helps remove some of the inhibitions to talking.

Couples, though, can be impossible with the telephone. For hours they can lie on the floor, sit in a chair, look out the window, read magazines, do homework, all the while they are talking to each other on the phone. Then, of course, after hanging up, they must call and tell their best friend about what's going on.

The phone plays an important role in dating and will always be a source of excitement for teenagers. But it can also be a problem-causer with parents. Many a family feud can be prevented by a wise, considerate teenager. Let me be sort of a mediator here. There is no sense in getting grounded or losing other privileges and having an unnecessary family blowout. Come onto middle ground and listen:

Time is the key. Parents, you don't mind if your young adults use the phone, do you? Of course not. What you object to is endless chatter, right? I have to admit that parents have a point. Sometimes the phone is like an addiction. Listen, help things go smoothly at home. Respect time limits. Be thoughtful of others who need to make calls or who are expecting them. Don't let telephone rules make you act like a mad bear being disturbed in winter hibernation. It just is not worth the friction it causes. Believe it or not, you will have plenty of opportunities to use the phone. That is, if you avoid snags with your folks.

Don't argue. One of the things that peeves parents most is listening to their teenager argue with a girlfriend or boyfriend on the phone. Fighting over the phone is especially bad because mere words can be misunderstood so easily. Besides, parents don't like to hear the bickering. Make a rule for yourself and stick to it: no phone fighting.

Avoid late calls. It can be very upsetting to parents when the phone rings late at night, and the call is for you. Especially if the caller is a member of the opposite sex. Put out the word: "Do not call me late [after such-and-such a time]." It will save on misery around the house.

The stuff so far will get you a little further through the dating maze, which up to now has been a difficult puzzle to solve. We have gotten past most of the dead ends and turned some key corners. But the next several chapters are the toughest part of the maze. The real pitfalls. Hang on tight!

An Inside Look:	Remind the people . . . to be peaceable and considerate . . . (Titus 3:2)
Beatitude:	*Happy are the considerate phone-users, for they will not be "dial-logged."*

30

Conversation

Have you ever feared not knowing what to say on a date? Have you thought, *What will we talk about?* When on a date do you start up the conversation—or do you wait for the other person to do it? Are you able to carry on a good conversation in a one-on-one setting? Are you shy or outgoing? When you talk, are you nervous or relaxed?

Good conversation is the key to exciting dating. Through talking we build a relationship. Whether or not a date was real fun often relates back to how much sharing was done. So those questions in the first paragraph are serious stuff.

Would you mind if I passed along some hints on how to have good dialogue? Here are seven ideas to improve your conversations:

Break the ice. Getting started is often the toughest part of good conversations. That's why we have time-tested catch phrases like:

"Nice day, isn't it?"

"How's your family?"

"How are you doing today?"

"What's been going on?"

"Have you done anything exciting lately?"

These are icebreakers. They get the ball rolling. Once you get started, everything seems to work itself out. Have you ever heard it said about a person, "He sure is shy-acting, but once you get him talking you can't get him stopped"? Most of us are that way. So have an icebreaker to open things up. And be original. Don't fall into the rut of using the weather to talk about. There are a million and one first lines. Try a question related to what you know interests the other person. Be imaginative. But above all—start!

Keep it upbeat. Too many young people drop into the darkest holes when they get together with friends or dates. Don't talk about how your parents bug you, or the things you can't stand about a teacher. Don't gossip about other people, or run down a classmate who has upset you. This is not a good influence on your date. It does not promote enthusiasm. It brings only a black moment into an evening or afternoon that should be dedicated to fun. Talk about positive things expressively. Be pleasant. Talk in friendly tones. Droning in a monotone is boring. You are a living, breathing human being with a vocabulary of thousands of words. Communicate!

Chitchat. Small talk about less than life-or-death matters is essential to warm conversation. Some call this the gift of gab. Of course, this is not all dating talk should consist of, but chitchat keeps things flowing. It can be about anything. Here are ten examples:

Last night's TV program

A funny joke you heard

A new fad that just started

Something funny that happened at school

Something you got in the mail

A book you just finished reading

A Bible verse you heard

Something that happened to your family

A new car you saw

Something your family pet did

Discussions. If you are with the right person, a good discussion can be fun. It helps pass the time driving to wherever you are going. It adds spice to a good dinner date. It gives you something to do while waiting for the ball game to start. A discussion can be about serious issues (abortion, capital punishment, a Bible truth, the economy) or about lighter matters (college, goals, friendship). Remember to be fair, because discussions involve opinions. Hardheads can end up in an argument.

Personal interests. It is fine to share personal hobbies or interests, okay to tell a little about yourself. But beware of telling your life story in one night. Some people are careless this way. They tell everything there is to know about themselves in one shot. Be selectively private. Share simple interests. Wait until you are older and dead serious about a person before revealing the mysterious total you.

Teasing. Some people seem almost made for teasing and even friendly sarcasm. A little of this can be fun, but—if overdone—can bring hurt feelings. Dole out your barbs carefully. That kind of "humor" can backfire.

Listen. Part of the key to good conversation is knowing when to be quiet. Trying to control the whole conversation makes the evening boring for the other person. There are times when silence is golden in conversation. Being a charming date is easy if you are a charmed listener at least part of the time.

Well, I think that's enough talk about talk. One last thing, fascinating conversation is the art of telling people a little less than what they want to know. One more last thing, the real art of conversation is not only saying the right thing in the right place, but also leaving unsaid the wrong thing at a tempting moment. One more last thing. . . .

An Inside Look: Let your conversation be always full of grace, seasoned with salt, so that you may know how to answer everyone.   (Col. 4:6).

Beatitude: *Happy is the conversationalist, for he/she brings dating to life.*

31

Rings and Things

Although "going steady" is an outdated term, it is not any different today from what it ever was. It still means that a guy gives a girl his ring, letter jacket, senior key, or any symbol that says there is some kind of commitment. It involves a mild agreement that promises not to date anybody else. It is a we-belong-to-each-other-only pact. Such an arrangement is like a contract with benefits for both parties, and it does have some nifty benefits.

You get the advantage of having someone who obviously cares about you. Who will listen to you. To whom you can tell your problems. Who accepts you the way you are. Who gives you gifts on special occasions. Who supplies dating security. Who gives you his or her family you can get to know and feel a part of. Who provides your first feelings of love.

Aren't those wonderful things? Sure they are. All of those things meet needs every person has. We all need to feel loved, to feel that we belong, to feel worthwhile and competent. We all want somebody available to talk to and be with. "Going together" fills the bill.

But there is something that confuses me. Why are so many couples going steady so young? After all, this is a semiserious step. Are they doing it only because it's the "in" thing to do? Because, listen, there are some bad side effects of dating one person steadily. Before you rush into what appears to be an innocent "love affair," you had better think about the problems that it causes:

It locks you down. At your age do you want to make such a binding commitment? Think of some great dates you might have to pass up. I know it's hard, but look ahead. Your future is only beginning. Watch several people in the twenty- to twenty-five age bracket. Those are the ones ready to tie themselves to one person and be settled. Do you really believe a fourteen-, or fifteen-, or sixteen-year-old is prepared for that kind of responsibility?

It usually causes sexual problems. The more familiar people of the opposite sex get with one another, the more the risk for sexual involvement increases. Don't be fooled into thinking you can "fall in love" with someone without wanting to satisfy that emotional feeling through physical contact. Maybe it doesn't happen in every case—just in ninety-nine out of one hundred.

It is hard to get out of the arrangement. The longer you date one person, the harder it gets to stop. The attachment gets very strong. Even if you want to break up, you can feel trapped and confused. You fear hurting the other person's feelings. Then you worry about not being able to get new dates. Finally, you fear what others will think and say. All this can be awful. It makes your stomach churn. You lose sleep. You lose your appetite. You cry a lot and fight a lot. Is this the way you want to spend your special years as a teenager?

I don't know about you, but when it comes to going steady, I vote thumbs down. Save the ring exchange for when you are really ready to mean it.

An Inside Look: Now we see but a poor reflection; then we shall see face to face. Now I know in part. . . . (1 Cor. 13:12)

Beatitude: *Happy are the free-daters, for they are always available to do what they want—no strings attached.*

32

Come-Ons

Flirting. That is the fine art of throwing and receiving passes and a very significant part of dating and attracting dates. From outright showing off to cool coyness, come-ons abound in the dating maze. But getting the reputation of being a flirt is not so terrific.

I don't know why, but it seems to be more acceptable for guys to flirt than girls. Maybe because most of a guy's flirting is joking around. Like the winking maniac. Or the one who makes eyes at all the girls. And have you heard some of their flirtatious one-liners?

"I woke up in love today, 'cause I went to sleep with you on my mind."

"Baby, where have you been hiding?"

"What's a beautiful girl like you doing in a place like this?"

"When I saw you I fell in love."

"I think I love you; what's your name?"

Crazy. But most of it is harmless, if people keep their heads on frontwards. Leave out the sexual innuendos and some flirting can be funny. After all, you have to let a person know if you're interested.

Anonymous admirers don't get many dates. That's why in frustration they finally cut loose and send a card or gift with "secret admirer" as the signature. This is a form of flirting, a way of building interest in the other person. There are some simpler ways:

Friendliness. Say something nice to the person whose head you are trying to turn. If the nut seems blind and you can't get his (or her) attention, find a slick way to talk to that person. Or just be friendly and pleasant. As the old saying goes: honey draws more flies than vinegar.

Compliments. That does not mean flattery, which is sickening. Don't go on and on. Just slip in a nice comment:

"I like your hair."

"You look extra nice today."

"I like that dress [shirt]"

"Don't you smell good today!"

Be smooth with this or it can leave a bad impression. That's why I say *slip it in*. Compliments that stick out like sore thumbs are embarrassing not attracting.

Smile. A sprite smile is irresistible. We all prefer smiling faces to blank ones. If you don't believe me, look at the faces on the covers of most magazines. You'll find they are smiling. A warm, pleasant smile can be very attractive!

Now don't turn into a flirting fool. A subtle, undercover come-on never hurt anybody, but a bold flirt comes off as pushy. If you think you have the hang of what I'm talking about, give me a coy wink . . . I mean a smile.

An **Inside Look:** Let us fix our eyes on Jesus, the author and perfecter of our faith. . . .   (Heb. 12:2).

Beatitude: *Happy are those who don't come off as come-ons, for big flirts get a lot of laughs but not many dates.*

33

Kissing

Candy Wessling and Klaus Wagher are world record title-holders. Their distinction in *The Guinness Book of World Records* is a strange one. In Springfield, Virginia, they held a smoochathon and kissed each other for 124 hours and 51 minutes. That's over five days!

Most teenagers would settle for five seconds, provided the kiss was with the right person. Kissing *is* much more exciting than holding hands. But even that isn't enough to satisfy after a while.

Don't get me wrong. I'm not saying that kissing is a sin. Actually, it's quite nice. Who doesn't dream of the exquisite softness lips have? So, if you have secret desires to try your mouth at kissing, congratulations—you're normal. You are not a sex maniac just because you are anxious for the thrill a kiss can bring.

However. . . . You were waiting for me to tack on a "however," weren't you? Okay, so I did. This is an important *however,* though. *However . . .* a soft, sweet, tender kiss is a special show of affection. It should not be treated like a cheap sideshow. Kisses should not be doled out like thirty-nine-cent hamburgers. They should be reserved for special moments.

Some people will kiss almost anybody anytime. Evidently they don't value their kisses very highly. Others feel as though they have to hand out kisses as payment for a date. Don't let this kind of pressure be put on you. A nice evening out does not require a show of affection. You don't owe anybody physical attention to "fulfill your obligation." If your companionship and friendship are not enough to make a date memorable, a kiss is not going to suddenly do the trick. In other words, spend more energy filling the evening with the unique you whom you have to offer instead of worrying about whether or not you are a good kisser.

A brief good-night kiss need not be a scene from *Romeo and Juliet*, but how long should it be? How many times should a couple kiss? It would be nice if God had come out with some clear-cut rules for situations like this. That would make it simpler. What the Lord wants, though, is for you to come to your own conclusions. He wants you to be sensible and make wise choices.

I think we can reasonably rule out long smooch sessions which invite passion to run high. Overstimulating your hormones is a fast track to trouble. Notice that I didn't say it had to be a kiss on the cheek, forehead, or hand. Nor did I say it had to be a peck. That does not mean I sanction "frenching" or marathons. Talk to your parents. Go ahead. They know what kissing is. Get their opinion.

"What if the guy who tries to kiss me is someone I don't want to kiss? What should I do?" That touchy question bothers many girls. "Awkward" is not a strong enough word to describe the tension of that situation. Try this. Reach out and put your hand on his shoulder before he makes his move. Pat him lightly and say, "Thank you for the nice date. Good-night." Then turn for the door. He'll get the message.

Which reminds me. Do your good-night kissing on the doorstep of your home only. Not in cars. And certainly not in public where the world watches. Nothing is as gross as a couple slobbering all over each other in crowded places. This safe home territory will also prevent further involvement.

May I ask one last favor? Please don't try to break Candy's and Klaus's weird record.

An Inside Look: An honest answer is like a kiss on the lips.   (Prov. 24:26).

Beatitude: *Happy are those who value their kisses, for they will be free and sensitive to share the niceness of a simple kiss.*

34

Petting

Now we get down to the brass tacks. That's the way it is with mazes. The farther in you go, the more complicated they get. Along these rocky cliffs, scores of teenagers take a painful fall. While what appears to be saturated with pleasure lures you closer, sometimes it is difficult to recognize the dangers.

How far should a couple go? Is it okay to give sensual massages? How about kissing the neck and ears? Are sexual touches okay, as long as clothes are left on? Is it wrong to pet to an orgasm? Is it acceptable to pet, so long as a couple doesn't go all the way? Wouldn't it be better to fool around and relieve the tension than end up in intercourse?

I've heard these questions, and their variations, a number of times. First I would like to answer them all by reminding you that your body belongs to God, if you have received Jesus Christ into your life. You are not your own. You are not free to use your body as you please without facing certain consequences. Always do what brings God glory with the body He has given you. Don't do anything that will cause guilt or make you ashamed to talk to Him.

My second answer to these questions is: what you begin doing you will most likely keep doing. You will not go backwards. If you pet sexually, you will do it again. What's more, you will be curious and excited to go a step beyond what you did last. Don't feed yourself that old I'll-only-try-it-once line. Once you start, it is almost impossible to stop. The flesh is weak. The flesh can't put up a fight. Feed it sensuality and you will create a monster.

Another point that should be considered is that petting seems to miss the spirit of morality. When Jesus talked about lust and fornication, He did not leave much room for moral impurity of any kind. There is no mention of ways to get quick thrills without blowing your virginity. If I get Him right, Jesus makes this pretty plain—sexual gratification belongs within the warm, loving relationship of husband and wife.

That's firing from point-blank range, and I don't like to do that. This is one area, though, where mincing words is for children. You are no longer a child. you have a body capable of doing adult things. So, girls, you must think ahead of time about what you will do when part boy/part octopus starts rubbing his hands all over you. If you are not ready, it is going to be an unforgettable night— in more ways than one. If you are prepared, it can be an unregrettable night.

Similarly, guys should make a pact with their hands. Teach those feisty wanderers to leave buttons alone, to leave blouses tucked in, to stay out from under skirts and sweaters, to leave belts and zippers belted and zipped, and to keep off private property. A gentleman exercises self-control. That alone will prevent most groping.

If you have the misfortune of dating a handsy ape, set him straight. Begin nicely by politely telling him, "No!" Then you could ease the pressure by suggesting you both go get a Coke. Anything to lighten the moment. If that doesn't abate him, a firm "Stop it!" is in order. Third time is "charm." Smack some sense into him and ask him to take you home! By the way, don't invite hands-on trouble by "teasing."

Darryl Royal, a noted college football coach, once remarked when asked about there being little passing in college football, "There are three things that can happen when you pass a football and two of them are bad."

His advice is explicit: when in doubt—run!

An Inside Look: Flee the evil desires of youth, and pursue righteousness, faith, love and peace, along with those who call on the Lord out of a pure heart.   (2 Tim. 2:22)

Beatitude: *Happy are those who confine their petting to the family cat, for they get scratches on their hands instead of their hearts.*

35

Let's Get Physical

I wonder how many of you flipped to this chapter first! How many, while glancing through the book, stopped here after seeing the title? Don't feel guilty if you did. There is a natural curiosity that you have about sex. Unfortunately, we live in a world that promotes unnatural superdrives toward the physical.

Some experts estimate that there are nearly eleven million sexually active teenagers in America. They estimate that nearly 80 percent of all boys and 67 percent of all girls under age nineteen have engaged in sexual intercourse. Some of this could be blamed on our sex-wild, permissive society.

But why do teenagers allow themselves to get so deeply involved? Why do so many create a mental, emotional, and spiritual torture for a brief chance at pleasure? Why do these millions risk the dangers of sex (pregnancy, venereal disease, personal guilt, and damaged self-image through a loss of self-respect)?

There are several reasons. Weigh them. Look at your own life. See if you fit into one of these areas. If you do, you are probably on the brink of sexual experimentation, or you may already be involved.

Unpreparedness. Some get into heavy physical activity because they did not anticipate the moment when temptation would come. They were not ready. Suddenly, there they were in privacy, turned on and unprepared to stop themselves. It just happened because they were not on guard. Soon they were trapped by the ravings of sexual impulse.

Inability to say no. Others have tried to make mental preparation, but when the time comes they allow themselves to get seduced by their own desires. They cannot say no, because their willpower has been drained. After a few defeats, they figure there is no sense putting up a fight. They reason that it is too late now, believing they have already blown it. Why try?

Popularity seeking. This is very sad. There are girls who think that by giving away sexual favors they will be well liked. To get attention, they make themselves available to the guys who can bring the most attention. Reputation goes down the tubes. So does self-respect. Frequently, girls caught in this quagmire agonize on the inside. A slow-growing hatred of self is building. To escape, they seek further sexual attention. But instead of feeling better, they end up feeling cheaper still. This horrible nightmare can leave lifelong scars.

To prove love. Don't fall for that old line, "If you really love me, you'll do it." Outside of marriage love and sex are rarely, if ever, connected. The truth is: "Love does not delight in evil but rejoices with the truth" (2 Cor. 13:6). Sex is not a proof of love; it is an act of marriage. Commitment is a proof of love. Be committed to purity if you believe you are in love.

I am sorry to say that there are guys who put pounds of pressure on girls to perform sexually. Girls who resist are often labeled "prudes" or "frigid." Some guys will not date girls who do not "put out." These tactics should never cause a girl to yield. It takes more courage to hold on until the time is right than to adopt the morals of an alley cat.

It is possible that some of you readers are in highly charged sexual relationships already. Maybe you are looking for a way out. I hope so. Do this. Pour out your heart to God. Receive the forgiveness only He can give. Then take action to prevent it from happening again. That could mean breaking off your current relationship, or else you might fall back into the snare. Even more so.

Whew! I'm glad this chapter is over. This is tense, heavy stuff
Who thought up this maze anyway?

An Inside Look: Marriage should be honored by all, and the marriage bed kept pure, for God will judge the adulterer and all the sexually immoral.   (Heb. 13:4)

Beatitude: *Happy are the teenagers who refrain from going all the way, for that trip should be reserved for a lifelong mate—then you never have to worry about coming back.*

36

VD

Venereal disease. Dreaded words. You probably have heard it called "the clap." Actually, there are several types of VD. All of them painful. Most of them curable with antibiotics.

We could sit around and giggle about the connotation of getting VD. We could be ostriches and jam our heads into the sand. We could make up filthy jokes and jive around about it. Or we could be mature and discuss a terribly disturbing issue. VD is a serious problem, and it relates very much to your age group.

Over 50 percent of all sexually transmitted diseases are contracted by young adults aged fifteen to twenty-four. How many does that figure to be? Well, here are the VD stats for 1980:

3,000,000 cases of trichomoniasis (infection of the vagina or male urethra that causes a discharge).

2,700,000 cases of gonorrhea (inflamation of the genital mucous membrane).

2,500,000 cases of nongonococcal urethritis commonly called NGU (infection of the urethra).

81,000 cases of syphilis (three-stage bacteria disease).

300,000 cases of herpes (both Simplex I and Simplex II are currently incurable. They are skin inflamations that recur frequently over a one-year period).

300,000 cases of pubic lice (causing itching skin irritation).

Medical experts estimate that there will be ten to fifteen million cases of VD reported this year. This means that anywhere from five to seven and a half million cases will occur in the fifteen-to-twenty-four age group! "The clap" is not a funny joke to snicker about in the school hallways or locker room.

It is estimated that over twenty million people now have herpes. It is at near-epidemic proportions. Herpes is believed to be related to causing cervical cancer. So it is time we woke up. The house is on fire!

I was listening to one of those call-in talk radio shows recently. The hostess was fielding questions from teenagers. One girl called to ask if the commentator thought it was wrong for girls to "sleep around." She answered yes and used VD as one of her reasons. Her words were shocking: "The more you sleep around, the greater the risk of getting VD. Sad but true. A lot of people out there have it, and they're the ones you'll be sleeping around with."

Oh, yes! I forgot to mention that doctors are growing in their concern over VD in even younger age groups. It seems the thirteen-to-fourteen-year-olds with this problem now number in the thousands.

There is only one sure way of keeping this from happening to you. Abstain. Besides, I've got a question for you. Doesn't it appear that God is sending a warning in direct relation to our society's permissiveness?

This is a gross, ugly subject. In fact, you may have skipped over this chapter several times before reading it. I can't blame you. It is a depressing topic to discuss! Necessary, though. You need to know that VD is *transmitted only sexually,* and that it happens to people your age every day.

An Inside Look: He satisfies my desires with good things, so that my youth is renewed like the eagle's. (Ps. 103:5)

Beatitude: *Happy are those who avoid VD, for they are the ones who have something to clap about.*

37

Feelings

The *Los Angeles Times* carried an unbelievable story a while back. A girl married the fellow who had robbed her at the beauty shop where she worked. Can you believe that? He still had to spend some time in jail! When questioned by reporters she answered, "It may not seem logical, but then it isn't logical. It's love."

How can a person tell if true love has come? Is it an emotional high? Is it a fast-beating heart? Is it an excited nervous feeling churning in your stomach? And while on the subject, can teenagers be in love? How old does a person have to be to experience love?

I think teenagers are capable of love. I also think a lot of so-called love is really infatuation. Love comes on several levels. There is *security love*, which brings warmth and closeness because one person keeps the other secure. There is the *sharing love* that exists between two people who have shared and experienced so much together they cannot imagine being apart. There is *inexperienced love*, where one loves another person because she or he has never had the chance at loving anybody else.

Then, there is *lasting love,* in which one learns that mutual love is being shared, and accepts the challenge of building on a solid foundation. Did you notice that? Lasting love means learning. Its partners do not *know*—they *grow.* And build. Lasting love is not temporary-minded.

Be honest. Most teenagers are not prepared for this serious a commitment. They do feel the emotional stirrings of love. Tender attachment and warm sharing add meaning to good relationships. But most first loves are not last loves.

In some cases, the love you experience at this age is great. Just don't get too tied down, or make ridiculous plans and promises you cannot possibly mean. Ward off the physical dangers. Most of all, be free to move on if and when the time comes.

Sometimes love boomerangs into hate. It happens. All of us get hurt. There is nothing that can prevent that. It is part of life and maturing. When someone does us wrong we have to shake it off. In spite of the insults and terrible things said in the heat of anger, it is important not to let terrible bitterness fester.

Have you ever met somebody full of hate? Maybe not, because most young people are good at forgiving and forgetting. Take my word, though, those who let hate get into them are a depressed bunch. Hate is like a cancer. It eats you up on the inside.

Healing damaged emotions takes good friendships, time, and help from the Lord. But dwelling on the hurt only makes it linger and spread. A good cry is okay—or punch a punching bag, or anything else on which you can take your frustrations out safely. After that is over with, unload the inner hurt on the Lord. He cares. Give Him a try. Still, all healing takes time.

Feelings are part of dating, both the ups and the downs. Both the loving glow and the crushing blow. You *will* make it through. Someday you might even look back on these impossible moments and laugh. Hard to imagine? Read this chapter again in about five years.

An Inside Look: A happy heart makes the face cheerful, but heartache crushes the spirit.   (Prov. 15:13)

Beatitude: *Happy are the tenderhearted, for they will be sensitive to the feelings of others.*

38

Fights

Can I let you in on a secret? When my wife and I were dating we used to make each other miserable with arguments. Stupid arguments! Know what's worse? They were almost always started by me. When I think back on my temper tantrums, I can feel my face stinging with prickly spurs of embarrassment.

I recall one of our shouting matches. To show you how dumb our arguments were, I can't even remember what it was about. I asked her to return all of the love poetry I had written to her. After storming out of her house, I tore them to shreds and threw them in the street. Over thirty cherished poems that could never be replaced.

I thank God for a tamed temper today. Looking back, I see now that some of it was lack of self-control, but most of it was childishness. Am I sorry for it? Yes, terribly. Am I ashamed of it? Very. There is no gold medal for being able to chew people out and tear them up on the inside. I would give anything to change those blots in my past. Praise God, though, now I have yielded my attitudes and emotions to Him. The Holy Spirit brings sweet peace.

Why am I telling this? Because you will get into a zinger of a fight someday, if you have not already. There is something in our nature that wants to get even, that lets anger boil up inside, that itches to tell somebody off, that wants to lash out when we think injustice has come to us.

Take it from a pro, who learned the art of fair fighting the hard way—there are better ways of straightening things out than having a war. Some confrontations are inevitable, so make a pact to follow the rules of fair fighting:

We will not fight when we are tired. Uncountable fights could be prevented between couples if they would obey this rule. When you are tired, your guard is down. Irritability is up. A few stray words can lead to disaster. Unnecessary disaster! Just say, "Hey, we're tired. Let's back off until tomorrow." Promise that if the problem still exists after a night of rest, it will be discussed the next day. You will find that a lot of things are lost and forgotten in sleep.

We will not raise our voices. Nobody listens to a screaming mimi. On top of that, once the tongue gets loose it is hard to corral. When both tongues get loose—hello, heartache. Raised voices promote the saying of things we do not really mean. We cannot take those things back, no matter how sorry we are.

We will listen to and consider both viewpoints. There are two sides to every coin. Sure, you are partial to heads (your viewpoint), but sometimes tails wins (the other viewpoint). Being hard-headed encourages more fighting. Hearing both perspectives is fair. Easily said, not so easily done. When the other person is talking, you will be tempted to jump in and interrupt. Don't. Things will be said with which you will disagree. Wait. Remember, the goal is to resolve the problem, not just to say your piece and then blow up.

We will make necessary apologies. "I'm sorry." Oh, those are difficult words to cough up. They seem to mean admitting failure and blame. None of us likes to be wrong, but upon occasion we all are. Learning early to apologize will help you in all of life's relationships. And even if you both agree that *you* are not at fault, apologize for any angry words—and forgive the other person.

If you expect to be perfect at these rules right away, think again. They take work. Above all, ask the Lord to take control of the face-off. Ask Him to soften your words and make tender your spirit. Then wrongs can be righted.

An Inside Look: He who guards his lips guards his soul, but he who speaks rashly will come to ruin. (Prov. 13:3)

Beatitude: *Happy are the fair fighters, because their words don't come home to haunt them.*

39

Breaking Up

Breaking up is hard to do. It is the last dark tunnel of the dating maze. If dating takes you on a roller-coaster ride of emotions, breaking up is the bottom of the track. When sex has been involved, it is even more complicated.

There are other reasons for breaking up besides sexual involvement. Some couples break up because they fight all the time. Different values can create a gap. Change of scenery is needed by others. A few relationships end because one person moves to a new location. Another cause is uncertainty—not knowing if the relationship is best anymore.

Whatever, if breaking up is in the script for you don't keep putting it off. Avoiding some pain and misunderstanding is impossible. Granted, having to be the one who says, "I think we need to date around," is no exciting prospect. But why stay in a lousy setup in which two people are unhappy?

Think it through. When you are sure the decision is correct, go with it. Take a deep breath and face that person privately, but confidently.

Be straight. Come right to the point. Beating around bushes is for monkeys and weasels. Say your piece in such a way that your decision must be honored. By the way, don't play breaking-up games, where the plan is to hurt the other person—to get even. Break up for sound reasons and give a straight explanation.

Be polite. Tact is an unfamiliar word, an even more uncommon trait. Tact involves smoothness in rocky situations. "Handle with care" is another way of saying it. Tact backs off from tearing hearts into shreds. It isn't weak, but gentle. Heartbreak Hotel sits at the end of Lonely Street, and for a while you will both be checking into its rooms. Splitting up on good terms makes your room tolerable and your visit shorter.

Stick with it. Regardless of threats (suicide, to turn friends against you, to run away, and so on), vows of eternal hatred, jabs of revenge, or pleas to give it one more try, stick to your guns. Nursing a half-dead relationship is pitiful work. You are at too glorious a time of life to waste it on a lame love. Teen years can never be relived. So make your breaks clean and move on.

All that is well and good, but what if someone breaks up with *you*? Won't that be a tough pill to swallow? You bet it will. Guess what, though! You won't die. Oh, you might feel like it for a while, but hearts mend.

At first you might be hesitant about new dates. Take your time. Rebound loves are a poor way to heal hurt. They create more problems than they are worth.

I think it is important for "victims" to accept the split. There are great things ahead! Looking back and moping are no help. Sure, I realize old memories creep out. That's okay. Just beware of the hoping-we-can-get-back-together-again syndrome.

One last thing, close your ears to sad love songs for a while.

An Inside Look: He has sent me to bind up the brokenhearted, to proclaim freedom for the captives and release for the prisoners. (Isa. 61:1)

Beatitude: *Happy are the teenagers who know when to step out of a relationship, for they escape a maze within a maze.*

40

Gift Giving

Hooray for holidays! I love to give gifts. Surprising people with a special present is one of my favorite pastimes. Giving is a grace and a joy.

Is it appropriate for young people to exchange gifts? I think so. Of course, one should not be motivated by obligation. Your heart has to be in it if the gift is going to be meaningful. We should not feel that we have to return a gift simply because we have been given one. Learn to allow others the pleasure of surprising you, too! Sometimes receiving is harder than giving.

Now to the matter at hand. What would make a good gift? That depends on the occasion. Also figure in how well you know each other. How much you have to spend is another consideration. Generally speaking, personal items are not appropriate gifts for daters. That includes things like expensive jewelry, lingerie, and most clothing items.

Here are some gift ideas. There are hundreds more, but maybe one of these will clear the fog on what to get.

Name plaque with name's meaning and, character reference

Good Christian book

Handmade items (they are priceless)

Dress gloves

Stationery

Inexpensive jewelry

Cologne

Good music (tape or record)

Magazine subscription

Key chain

Leather belt

Gift certificate for clothing

Flowers

Customized T-shirt

Personalized notepads, pens, jewelry

Chocolates

Unique poster or wall decoration

New Bible with name engraved

Pen and pencil set

Something of sentimental meaning to the two of you

You may already have your own ideas. That's fine. Have fun with them but keep gifting in perspective. Don't go into hock. Extravagance often misses the beauty of giving. The old saying, "It's the thought that counts," is still true. Naturally, the gift counts, too. All the more when it has that "from me to you" touch.

What's that I see up ahead? Is it a light at the end of the tunnel? Are we finally going to find our way out of this maze? I believe so, and it is right here in this unlikely chapter that we find the map to show us the way.

The key to successful dating is giving a gift. The gift is *you*. Fulfilling dating means sharing your faith, your goals, your dreams, laughter, tears, and friendship. It is giving your faults along with your strengths, because they are part of you, too. Be lavish with the simple you—with conversation and silence, with personal insights and fine-tuned listening, with ingenuity and originality. What a gift that will be! Believe me, though, if you date this way, you will receive more good times than could ever be given in a single gift.

Draw closer now and see the guiding light. Maps are no good without light. But what is that light? It is not a what—but a He! And He is Jesus. The Light of the World is also the Brightest Lamp to light your dating path.

What could be more *amazing* than that?

An Inside Look: Thanks be to God for his indescribable gift! (2 Cor. 9:15).

Beatitude: *Happy are the gift-givers, for they remind us of love's greatest gift—Jesus Christ.*